HERE TO DARE

HERE
TO
DARE

10 GAY BLACK POETS

ARTHUR T. WILSON
JOHN D. WILLIAMS
ROBERT WESTLEY
HAROLD MCNEIL ROBINSON
CRAIG A. REYNOLDS
STEVE LANGLEY
CARY ALAN JOHNSON
DAVID WARREN FRECHETTE
DON CHARLES
DJOLA BERNARD BRANNER

Edited by Assotto Saint

1992   GALIENS PRESS   NEW YORK, NY

Typeset by The Kenton Company
P.O. Box 6909
New York, NY 10150

Printed in the United States by McNaughton & Gunn, Inc.
P.O. Box 2070
Ann Arbor, Michigan 48106

This a trade paperback original from Galiens Press,
Box 4026
524 West 23rd Street
New York, NY 10011

First edition, first printing: November 1992

Library of Congress Cataloging-in-Publication Data

Here to dare : 10 gay Black poets / Arthur T. Wilson ... [et al.]. —
     1st ed.
          p.   cm.
     ISBN 0-9621675-2-5 : $10.00
          1. Gay men—Poetry. 2. American poetry—Afro-American authors.
3. American poetry—20th century. 4. Afro-American gays—Poetry.
5. Gays' writings, American. I. Wilson, Arthur T., 1945-
PS595.H65H4 1992
811'.540809206642—dc20   92-20026
                                                    CIP

Photo of Arthur T. Wilson by Mel Wright; of Harold M. Robinson by Beckett
Logan; of Craig A. Reynolds by Robert Giard; of Steve Langley by Jason M.
Johnson; of Cary Alan Johnson by Leigh Mosley; of David Warren Frechette
by Robert Giard; of Djola Bernard Branner by Barbara Sansome.

In loving memory
of fellow poets:
Rory Buchanan
Bland J. "BJ" Carr
Craig G. Harris
Donald Woods
and sister street queens:
Cecil
Marsha "Pay Them No Mind" Johnson

I can move, move, move any mountain.

The Shamen

TABLE OF CONTENTS .

ACKNOWLEDGMENTS

I wish to thank the ten contributors for sharing their writings and making this collection possible.

In addition, I wish to thank the following individuals for their encouragement and assistance: Oye Apeji Ajanaku, Akhenaton, Thom Bean, Michael Cummings, Thomas Glave, Kenton Grey, Essex Hemphill, Walter Holland, Michele Karlsberg, Carl Morse, Pedro Perez, Charles Michael Smith, Vega, and Phill Wilson.

I also wish to thank my life-partner Jaan Urban Holmgren for his constant support and love.

Assotto Saint
Editor/Publisher

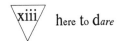

HERE TO DARE

arthur t. Wilson

NAKED EARTH SONGS

ARTHUR T. WILSON completed several academic degrees at New School College, New York University, and the University of London at Bedford. He received numerous academic scholarships, including the Martin Luther King, Jr. Scholarship for graduate work at NYU. He is listed in *Who's Who in the East*, *5,000 Personalities of the World*, and other biographical monographs. Poet, playwright, and teacher, waiting for the moment when human beings cut the crap with pigeonholing everything. The poems in this collection have appeared on stages throughout New York and have been danced, sung, shouted, and brought to life by all those friends that continue to help him WRITE ON!

"My collection of poetry is dedicated to my parents, Mr. and Mrs. Elmer Wilson, Chico Kasinoir, and all those brothers and sisters that have moved heavenward in the struggle for equality, justice, and humanhood. ACHE!"

here to dare

Naked earth songs sing everywhere —
The bloody book is never closed.
From pyramids to bombs,
From herbal healings
To concrete cities
Packed with screams
Held back,
And SCREAMS LET OUT....

Knowledge deficient of logic
Or common sense.

Where are we?

From necessary gods
To NO GOD —
Where are reasons
To live life wisely?

Instead, it's panic
Hatred — zombies masquerading new frontiers —
It's unattended starvation eating
Through the brains of babies
With no more tears;
It's carnival rhythms
Chained up in wars;
It's YOU and me BLEEDING,
NEEDING,
While life recedes.

Naked earth songs
Everywhere.

arthur t. Wilson   18

Men with leering eyes, wildly mingle
Under the elusive dim light.
And a body-game of magnetic lust rages
Against the sordid roulette
Of selecting a momentary rose.

Grabbing for air,
A motley bouquet of greedy fingers
Performs a lost tango in the shadows.
SORRY, DON'T KISS. MAKE NO MARKS.

Hands, so many pulling and stroking hands.
Then, someone is sized up as a thorn
And rejected by the peeling X-rated film booth,
While others masturbate to whiffs
Of amyl nitrate as a rock'n'roll jukebox
Blasts into the dogging scene.
Stale desperation stalks to prey on anything
Moving. Hands!   SO MANY HANDS!

Like Last Supper maggots,
An octopus of desire
Waits in the corner for a SOMETHING, ANYONE
Willing to give up his juice.
Circles of circling people pull
To investigate a hand that might push away
With a No! NOT ME! I'M JUST RESTING!
I'M WAITING FOR A WHITE BOY! A BLACK BOY!
MY FANTASY PLEASING!
                                    SWISHING
There are all types. The ~~switching~~ sissy,
Lips perched, giggling for attention.
Then there is the butch bullet

Through calculating eye, who tells you
He's only after the make-believe mirror image
Of his phony self. Also ride down
The pot-bellied, the confused, the lost,
The old sweet wrinkled men hoping for youth,
A little, from a touch gained through
A cherished bargaining —
There are so many HUNGRY men, circling
For reasons not to feel uncommon, QUEER,
Or thrashed among the cheap thrills of semen
Dripping down musty stalls.

Backroom roses, what kind of roses are these
Backroom kind? Taking a sly vacation
From a lover, or family, or wife?
Some terror-stricken — O God,
If someone should notice me —
Readily avoiding the openness
Upon which the heart will sing.

Over there! Over there! OVER THERE!
One beauty rides his horse down on a scream
Of lustful joy until, UNTIL THE ENTIRE ROOM
Becomes a perspiring crunch of jealous onlookers.

A few manage a smile, pressed against the walls,
The busy walls of histrionic seductions. Some
Just cum, zip up their pants, and head home
To sip brandy, Coke, or tea. And most,
Turned down all night, keep balancing fantasy
Against the sizzle of available prime night heat.
Until tired of going through changes,
They wipe off their hands on their pants.
The quick exit, turning the corner,
Usually hoping to forget that momentary rose
That refused to move from the darkness.

arthur t. Wilson   20

An alluring HELLO. Perhaps spirits rise.
I'll call you up and you'll wonder who I am!
And even I might not be quite sure
If you're the one that left my shoulder tattooed
With a raw circus of bites.

I might also not be sure if you're the one,
THE ONE who turned back long enough to say:
DON'T, PLEASE DON'T CALL ME
AFTER 11 O'CLOCK!
MY ROOMMATE GOES TO BED EARLY.
MY MOTHER GOES TO BED EARLY.

Numbers. Names. Names on business cards
Or finely printed on old matchbook covers.
I suppose that like a pilgrim
I keep imagining my cards can one day
Be called upon to form a fort against
The need to need.

We who think that night
And need are both the same
Have so many little scraps of paper
Stuffed whimsically into wallets
Or safely tucked into bureau drawers.

Names. I have to remember
To write beside a name:
"Thin shoulder blades," or "This one had a mole
Along the left side of the stomach."
I must devise some identifying clue
So that when I make all those calls
I'll know who I'm calling.

You see, saving little scraps of paper
And knowing that they will remain just that
Not transferred into books of addresses
Or indexed neatly into a file —
SAVING LITTLE SCRAPS OF PAPER
Is a kind of mental masturbation
Good to no one.

Not even good to those of us who think
That the inside of matchbook covers
With numbers is a kind of insurance.
Nor can we seriously expect a proper settlement
When the accident of being caught
With our own selves
Overtakes us in some bar, disco,
Or alleyway where loneliness lines the walls
Of yesterday's wailing laments of
So many pieces of paper.

AN ALMOST HAIKU BROTHER POE-UM

For Bill McClenin

Meet you
In a sky house blue,
And share each paradise
Where everything necessary
Is never misconstrued.

Please don't call me
Shaking pain loose like a mangy dog
Just bathed and hating the water.
Please, cleanse all filth
From your essence, and live.

Please don't call me
Shifting through bad-news hieroglyphics
Until rueful rivers of negative tensions
Make the wallpaper peel from the walls.
Resist such pathetic chatters
And devotions you never had.

Please don't call me
Falling apart for the sport of it,
Masquerading nightmares with a boost
When rarely few of your words share honesty.

Please don't call me
Projecting superiority
From discarded diaries and resentments.
Please don't call me
To tell me you are the only one
Cleaning off karma, and searching
For eternity's gentler light.

Please don't call me
Unless you want to inform me
That you died yesterday, or grew up,
Or found a glad-heart reason
To be the gingerbread sweetness
Or diamond you are.

SPILLING NECESSARY BRIDGES

For Guillermo Gonzalez

Indelible,
Determined,
Standing eagle-like
Near the wading pool descent
Of my solitary life,
Learning to discard
The intentional and perfect lies
That confine lifeblood gambles,
I fly inside your soul's phoenix,
Spilling necessary bridges —
The crossing, merely excited extensions
Gleaned from falls or hunch once concealed.
Seeking earth I still fly through the windows
Of everything, where I may scream and stumble
On the edge of the yeast, cauldron of repeated fears,
Knowing not where to locate a love-pledging place
To lay the parading image bulk of my aching head —
But there is no godparent, nor magical moment
That will arrive to guide us with lotus and moons.
It is just you and me, spilling necessary bridges.

arthur t. Wilson

24

I

There are impelling planets in my mouth,
A lover-proof furnace inside my soul.
Yielding, all my ingredients ancestral,
Furious, and I can't sit down.
Life isn't just about a pretty face
Or how many centimeters a dick is.
Better hold on to the oasis of yourself.

II

A fine juju sorcery the shoreline of your lips,
I think you saw God but only share the crust.
Yes, I am bathed in creation's paradoxical
Song, and there is no way to keep
Yourself clean underneath such filthy
Liars, backstabbers, and sinking wits.
I'm an abandoned building without heat
And living there. I'm a fantasy behind
A parked truck until I go mad and slap
My damned self. Or I'm anybody's lover
Until the plot thickens, and sympathy is
Dumped for the next jungle sweet.

III

Mudslide in my shoes.
Knew I shouldn't have returned
To your cold pouting apartment,
Having to sleep on the floor
Next to your new pet acquisition.
I had split from a bird-cage existence,
Opera, and antique oppression things.
This pet hadn't received the keys
Yet had already been written into your WILL.
While I was the analyst-ghost,
The comedian, an immediate kindness
Across everyday's clock,

Pushing back your wrinkles.
And it was I who held you back from jumping
Out of the window or having a face-lift.
Tonight you have your new electric,
I have my pulled-out hair,
My itchy ass, and a curse for you.
Yesterday I passed by the ditch
And you weren't there; I cried all day.

IV

O.K. Motherfucker!
Who threw the baby out with the trash?
And who stole my heart last year
While having a mental breakdown
On the A train? New York has become
Too small. Sometimes I walk into a room
Or a movie theater, and it seems
Like almost everyone has had my ass.

V

Can't grease yourself like a pig no more.
Can't grease yourself like a pig no more.
Yesterday I passed by the ditch
And you weren't there; I cried all day.

(Cecil was a homeless troubadour who resided in Greenwich Village for several decades. He was crazed, volatile, alluring, and an instant diary of conscience, relevant to those who dared listen to his song).

arthur t. Wilson   26

IN MEMORIAM
(RED CLOUDS FOR JIMMY HALL)

Sometimes, I do not wish that anything be a poem.
For the weight from savoring a lost emotion
Inside memory clots the brain,
And can crease even a hard man's rock
Into crumbling recognition: Pain.

Jimmy, Cecil is out in the hall.
He wants to read his "Hello Operator
No I Won't Accept Reverse Charges."
In a second his poem will be over,
And Cecil will be passed out on the streets
With fleas on his donkey, and fragile dreams
Swimming through crazed eyes — another piece
Of shopping bag amusement amidst a fraternity
Of decaying city blight.

The buffalo woman in the unemployment line
Looks at me, her radar orbiting.
She wonders what I'm thinking.
My face must be twisted up. And if I told her
That I was thinking of Jimmy,
She'd probably say, I KNEW IT!
WHERE ARE ALL THE MEN?

A frantic crippled woman
Also on the unemployment line,
Swings through her crutches, smiling, laughing,
Until some bovine supervisor with plastic concern
And dandruff offers a LIGHT MAINTENANCE JOB
LIFTING SMALL BOXES, THAT'S ALL.

SELL TUPPERWARE, someone wails out,
THAT'S HOW I GET OVER.
THE PROBLEM IS I KNOW MY RIGHTS,
The crippled woman says, I KNOW MY RIGHTS.
I ALWAYS WANTED TO BREAK INTO SHOW BUSINESS.
MAYBE THEY'LL OFFER ME A JOB AS A ROCKETTE!

Jimmy, racism is hawking inside
With its eternal roundup of poison
And the dead-end streets that I'm still on.
I see only hard eyes.
Snarling snares of despondent people
Are piling up all around us.
Sacrifices everywhere, but FOR WHAT?

A man at the Port Authority Bus Station
Goes down the up escalator backwards,
Throwing kisses to an imaginary person,
Telling *her* not to watch television
For it would rot *her* brain.

Two ragged winos spar.
Blood spurts from lice-infested heads.
Guard dogs sit. Cartoon police
Discuss LOTTO and NIGGERS.

Stale cake and several elastic young men
Watch the men's room door, suggesting
Through a model's pose, that someone's night
Can easily be fulfilled if the game is right.
A man dressed in leather asks for a cigarette,
His hat mashed down to the side — And I say
JIMMY, just like that.

Why couldn't that man be you... standing next
To the heat duct where congregations of bag people
Huddle to sleep warm and pray for angels?

One electric bag woman sitting
On crushed bundles, writes her memoirs.
She tells us that she's going to be FAMOUS
BY MORNING and receive FLOWERS
FROM THE PRESIDENT

ALTHOUGH HE'S A SON OF A BITCH.
She then tells us she shouldn't urinate
On herself because it's not nice
And it smells bad.

A bouncing jack-in-the-box goon offers her
A donut. DON'T YOU UNDERSTAND?! she screams,
Throwing the donut in the air,
I'M NOT BEGGING, I'M FINISHING MY BOOK...
BEAT THE DEVIL RUNNING.
AND WHEN I FINISH IT, I'M GOING TO BE ON TV.
IS ED SULLIVAN STILL ON?

On the subway death, a young Black man
With pants up to his groin
Smiles and turns a pearl or two.
He extends an envelope,
His face pleading smoothly for help
To purchase a new artificial leg.
WHAT'S WRONG WITH THAT LEG, JACK?
Someone snarls out, TIMES ARE ROUGH
AND YOU HAVE TO LEARN HOW TO MAKE DO.
Smiling, an angelic spirit
In green sneakers and chocolate wood
Moves down the subway death anyway,
Begging and falling into indifference.

No matter which way I turn,
Water or bird — competing only with myself —
Hispanic workers out-of-brown-bag-laughter,
Splashing down beer,
Dismiss so easily the surreal face of America's
Circus trails. I too must learn this fire.

Jimmy, after another poetry reading is over,
And everyone still casts suspicions,
Numbness, or blame — all the slippery
Metaphors and images spent —

here to dare

I saw your face in the crowd,
Bidding goodbye to this selfish race.
Jimmy, ain't nothing but red clouds
All over the place,
And nobody knows which way to turn.

NEVER GIVE UP

Never give up.
For we have had
Strong fathers,
Courageous, creative, tormented,
Angry, universe strivers —
Providers.

Fathers never gave up.
Had tightrope justice
Racist intrusions,
Oppression's trick-bag images,
Cornbread, mothers' tears,
And super-dick expectations
To leave brown babies
All over ghetto linoleum
In American cities
That called them "nigger"
And choked off dreams.

Fathers,
Whether irresponsible
Or out of control,
Went nowhere gracefully,
And went everywhere
As revolutionary notes
In a book that holds
Everyone's name.

john d. Williams

THE BLUE EARTH: POEMS

JOHN D. WILLIAMS lives and writes in East Orange, New Jersey.

AIDS:
CONSIDERATIONS OF FEAR

because i do not want to tell you
about the many men i did not know
who touched me,
when you ask me if i am afraid,
my mouth stutters into silence —
i do not even know who they were.

i can tell you
that there were hands not afraid
of my entire body —
and that i, my feelings/my person
and my entire self
were shaped against/within
the meanings of those hands,
and for the touch of those hands,
i am without fear.

now when i awaken alone,
the morning light breathes
against the bareness
of the walls of my sleep
in inklings of the imagined self.

memory elaborates
in renewed belief.

nothing will be
as beautiful
to me
as you are
next to me
asleep.

the circles
that you make in your sleep
are to me like the despair
of these trees in september,
tossing the wind
along the street
at midnight.

my feet turning into sand
as if i were at the beach,
this is a dance —
the nearness —
that i have waited for.

if i am sleepless these nights,
it is because even beyond the random violence
that snaps like an electric terror,
it has been dark for so long
that the body and the feelings
cringe in sharp angles
against the considerations
of touch —

and until you have said no,
i will continue to come
and follow this silent sleep-dance
through the night
where our arms
and.fingers
meet and clasp
in the dark.

here to dare

when you asked,
i could not explain the sadness,
other than to say
that you did not understand —
i can explain now.

it is not as if we are actually bleeding
(the unchartered night tumbling
from our mouths like sea stars),
nonetheless the spoken language
litters before our steps
like red peonies —
the body ululates
like a tenor saxophone,
the sum of our beauty
rubbing against the flesh
like shutters.

it is october now...

loneliness is not a difficult thing
in october —
the silence
like a perennial light,
the sun reaches
through the window
like hands.

bronze delineations
accumulate across the face.

i am not helpless
when i talk about need,
when i talk about my feelings
in tinted reflections of men
who disappear at touch.

it is simply like that sometimes...
but what do you care? —
you are not holding my hand.

at the door to my heart
are my suitcases
on either side of the door
like shadows —
that is what the music
is really all about:

the meaning is melody
and i can tell you about melody:

> the midnight rain
> revelling before the feet
> like red october,
> the air sings.

> as if for the first time
> love and hunger
> are discovered again new
> and i am returned to myself...
> in the shiftings of my voice
> and limbs
> i enact myself,
> scattering these sounds
> from my mouth
> like milkweed
> in an afternoon light.

in melody
i can speak
for what is beauty
among the wreck —
bright pebbles silver the air
like the aura
of a full moon.

PRIVATE POEM 2

in the blue pastel
beneath the street lamp,
the falling leaves tatter
against the wind
like dying stars
in the darkening october night.

soon the season will be snow.

the air is full
of voices.

THELONIUS MONK:
WHERE MEMORY AND DREAMS COLLIDE

the night is photographed
across the sky
in forgetful expansions of place.

slow deanimate conjectures
pressed from the soft shadows
of these night-frames,
against these strictures
we continue to dream.

the language of our listening
faltering in unsteadied voicings
of who we are/who we might have been,
the clattering definitions
of manufacture
take precedence in this ritual reproportioning
of space and meaning —
our names slipping away
like unrecognized soundings
of discontent,
our willingness to love disappearing
like the vanishing wetness
of this unforeseen night rain.

there are continuative dimensions
of this experience/
                    this knowing...
propelling the instance of our meaning
through gathering circles of increasing light,
we reiterate the connectivity of souls
moored in consequence with earth
and tethered upward against these limits
of night.

the work is to be done —
my fingers remark upon the unnamed grief.

there is the moment
of this midnight hour
in which i imagine unaccustomed love...
the dream that we are
who we say we are —
this night of the moon
traveling a trajectory
all its own.

PRIVATE POEM 3

as if the darkness
were in pieces,
the night cloaks the room
in mirrors.

to have imagined love
and never have understood:

this night aura
clinging to my hands
from my body:

love.

it is said
that i am lost
in the music
that i am dislocated
in melody,
but dislocated i am not
and nonetheless dislocated
i am —
in transcribing the meanings
of this place
to an inhabitable place
against the tyranny/the legacy
of incessant grief.

kansas city blows
through my horn
like sand
and i come to the place
of melody —
i am no stranger
to travel.

the silence and the sea
through the ears
like the same sound,
there is the delight
of these random colors
across the face —
into some more lyrical site,
in the silence
the lady and i
were like twins.

draft winds blow steeply
across the body.

the instruments of earth
should reiterate kindly
upon the body
the journey of stars.

orange and blue feathers
spiral brightly
in the light.

PRIVATE POEM 6

the urgencies
wrapping around my heart
follow me through the streets
like sirens.

at home
the door is crowded
with phantoms,
their hands
around the inside frame
like pressed flowers.

i would have stayed
with you
anywhere.

because you are a dancer
i knew that you would understand
when i said
that in order to make language
i am dancing with death —
the darkness pirouettes
in the imagination
like leaves.

that i speaking of memory
should have forgotten
so many things
is not where we should be
at all.

somewhere
it must be more beautiful
than this —
a sudden discovery
that the room
is in flames.

i am alone
and for the pain inside
there is nothing to be said,
nothing to be done —

the afternoon travels
across the face
like rain.

the dull-yellow of these leaves
at autumn's end
rains quietly through the window
in this gray light
of noon.

to have been left
without words
is a tragic way
to end a love affair.

speak to me
when you leave.

OCTOBER LETTER

it is as if the brittle autumn season
were a melody —
the burnished tones settling
like fallen leaves,
the body transported
in time and space.

and what i think i have been trying to say
is that there is everywhere around us
a disilluminating grief
that will not be stilled/
that is not the center of things —
everywhere we reappear to one another
in electrified distortion.

this season is like the window/the door
through which all things pass
and as we (in our instance)
record the soul's memory —

john d. Williams

pressing against this extraordinary confusion,
in the october light
the heart finds more room
than it had imagined to exist
in time and space.

it has been difficult to say this,
to admit that i am saddened
by the sight of the world —
the vagaries of wealth and poverty,
of life and labor —
it matters little who is listening,
who understands —

in the october fire,
the earth/the air/the light
are attuned to these urgings to life
through the door —
and one binds upon oneself
as if one were understood.

whether or not this or that
is understood so clearly now,
there is still melody.

the bop dissonances
that alter the fabric of melody
in my ear
run through my fingers
as if my fingers and these sounds
were in love —
memory surfaces
in my hands
like sea nets.

there is something present
that is not the music,
but who am i to query?

things change,
they always have.

robert Westley

NOT WITHOUT SORROW

ROBERT WESTLEY was born in New Orleans in 1962 and lives in San Diego, California. He attended the New Orleans Center for Creative Arts as a high school student, and maintains his interest in creative writing, especially poetry and short prose pieces, while pursuing a career as a philosopher-cum-lawyer-cum-community activist. His writing has appeared in *The Road Before Us*.

To Paul

LOOKING BACK ON A TIME

Looking back on a time
Before there was time to look back upon
I do not know
If the grass was green
Or brown and withered
I cannot tell
If there was an apple tree to climb
A neighbor's pet to frighten
A toy or a friend
Small faded clothes found in boxes
They aren't mine
They were never mine
I can't remember
Who that small child is
I see in a picture
Yellowed and grayed
Is that me
No I am myself
The strange child in the picture
He who is not me but is
Did he possess my first thoughts
Know everything I was and did and am
And if that forgotten person
Can be lost in so few years
In many more years
Will I forget myself?

Robert Westley

MY MEMORY OF GRANDMOTHER

In the rumble of her throat-clearing
I felt the earth tremble
As when ten thousand gazelles go galloping
From the lioness who stalks
In the broad light of day.

FATHER

It was you who burned
The dead leavings of autumn
Before the wind could take them.
You gathered the world
Into one rusted drum filled with fire.
Your hair and skin
Smelled of smoke, of carbon.

You cleared the way
Like a deacon preparing for eternity,
A pharaoh building his tomb.
Winter came and I was ignored.
You drank the snow — your face
Changing into a carapace of stiff nerves.

And now winter sits on us
Like a heavy cold iron.
Father, we must leave this land,
These rituals, the fire.
I feel myself becoming you,
You becoming air.

here to dare

He does his act
Like a tightrope walker
Each step measured
Each step circling on disaster
Each heartbeat
Louder than the last.
If he falls there is a sound —
Wind being blown on tinfoil.

His act is done
Like a circus clown's.
First applause, then laughter
Then watchful patience —
The audience expecting magic
As their children do.
His smile is worn
Either up or down
Depending on experience.

His act is in theory
A master of ceremonies'.
Woman hanging head down from a rope
Spins like a glittering spider
Man balancing china cups like a seal —
He describes their worlds
Which exist in a circular universe:
Being a part
And yet removed.

They say that friends who one another keep
Forever, never sleep together.
But who are they to say
What measure proves my love for you?
Or that we must forbear to do
As mind and heart incline
And sleep apart?

In solitude and pain I pass
Nights and days obedient
To a dogma neither expedient
Nor right, nor true. What for?
To preserve us as we were before
Misfortune beggared both our hearts
And made us sleep apart.

Come now, dear friend,
Before we reach the end,
I will show how life begins anew
For paupers such as me and you.
Or stay apart. Forever
Loved and yet untouched
By a friendly heart that feels too much
Pain to see your beauty
And remain unmoved.

I REMEMBER THE NIGHT

I remember the night we swam among the fish
That fed us, and the curving sky
Spread like our table with silver and onyx.
I remember mother-of-pearl
Crushed beneath our palms,
And the taste of sea salt
On your shivering blue lips.
I remember, as you stood above the waves
Your hair glistening with brine,
Your skin slick and shiny as whalebone,
Your eyes like salamander.
I remember you would turn to me,
Serene and hypnotic, and smile —
Like an invitation to immutable joy,
A way of never letting go.

SITTING ON BERKELEY STEPS

I waited for you all day
Here among the multi-colored throngs
Busy about their lives.
I am the invisible idler
The dreamer unseen by eyes
Sharply attuned to the changing attitudes
Of the sky, a sudden vision
Of a much-missed friend.
Jewel-laden tables line the streets
Of this bazaar like small ships
Navigating a rough sea.
Each stroller crashes by.
Desire, like a wave, rises
And falls, while young beautiful men
Adjust their profiles
Against the sun.

THE PUB

O Commissioner of Booty in New Haven
I'd like to talk to you.
I heard that you're the last big-dick
White boy — something like a Rotwurst.
Tell me where I apply
For an apprenticeship in groping.
My credentials are exemplary:
I am thin
I am beautiful
I am horny as hell
I eat cock on a whim
And my long black fingers are sticky
With lust.
So tell me, please
Who do I have to drink with
To get a fuck around here?

AFFECTION FOR A GOD

Little Mr. God
With your arrows full of lust
Your aquatic eyes
Your petal skin
Your mania for fire
If I could
I would eat you
And spit love in everyone's face.

All night long I held my boy
Whom I picked up in the cafe/bar
Anderes Ufer which is not far
And where often I enjoy
Schokolade topped with cream
Or coffee while I read my book
Pretending not to really look
As the beauty with torn jeans
Bends over to adjust his cuff
Or pulls blond hair back to light
His cigarette and starts to write
With lust my glances are enough
For intrigue to disturb the air
Of sweet indifference on his face
That loud displays could not erase
In this place where boys are fair
But cool so ever cooler than
Sex requires to get a man.

CIRCUMCISED PENISES

If you cut the tip of a cucumber
And rub it before peeling
You get the fever out.

HYMN TO PASSION IN TIME OF PLAGUE

The drone of music twists and flaps
Like laundered sheets on a clothesline
In the wind. My heart leaps up like jazz
Sudden, seductive — inviting you to touch
All of me in you dreaming —
Rejuvenated by the beauty of hands
And buttocks, and lips, and penises.
Remember always voices bathed in wine
Rising like cicadas above speaking.
Our limbs relaxed by love
We intertwine tongues whose buried breath
Beats the ambiguity from my glance.
Now is the time to be honest, and naked
And close beneath sheets dark with sweat.
Folding back taut skin in a storm of dance
Our movements are so deft, so delicate
We never notice our souls
Like heavy rain
Move down in death.

LINES
(FROM BERLIN)

Chocolate is for luxury
When I am very poor. Smoking
To remind me of my death. Both
Joy and sadness drinking. And love
When I can get it, to stay alive and beautiful.
Forever young.

Ideas memories images like the time I stepped on a nail and bled for four days on my sister's freshly waxed floor but consequently did not die which proved a disappointment death being a mysteriously enticing prospect like putting your finger in a flame until it begins to sizzle and then picking at the burned skin after first dousing it with ice or water or butter or whatever your particular remedy is for there are many and some I've discovered can be quite delightful feel that sound wash through your mind like the smell of expensive chocolate or the smoke from a cigar delightful which reminds me of sashay or concupiscent words I love with all my heart but can never find a use for like memorized poetry and empty wine bottles and old notebooks that plague me every year with uselessness which brings me back finally and forever to this subject of idealism memorabilia imagination and not thinking in this vast world of the ordinary where blood only blood munificent blood will turn blind eyes around blood that precious sauce that watery equalizer that stuff of dreams that blue sand that green preserver that red salve blood: dream on it....

QUESTIONS CONCERNING
THE FATE OF A KIND OLD WOMAN

Why has the kind old woman in the indigo dress hidden herself behind a gum tree she who has never in her life had occasion to slap a mosquito and who has always been the kindest of mothers to her 2,486 children and who has never had a violent thought except when she was blinded while stealing lemons from a fat and greedy aristocrat who had her husband killed for smiling on Sunday and then her anger was only in jest because she really did not like her husband he never paid her alimony after their divorce and had in fact demanded that she pay him wages for giving her so many adorable children whom she loved very much but did not receive love in return because they realized they all were bastards and their true father was a fat and greedy aristocrat named Igor who never smiled on Sunday and liked blinding his mistresses especially their mother whom they hated and for no particular reason except that she forced them to watch while she viciously beat her dog with an indigo stick?

What has the old woman done with the indigo stick which matched her dress her hat her shoes and her purse and with which she at last murdered her poor little dog who was indeed evil and some say mad for it was reported to have bitten an aristocrat named Igor who at once became unfaithful to his wife and began murdering men who smiled on Sunday and rightfully so for it is a well-known truth that men who smile on Sunday are bound by fate to divorce their wives and leave them with 2,486 hateful children and a very mean dog who bites aristocrats on the ankle and must finally be beaten to death by their mistresses even though this is illegal according to the laws of men and God because murder is a form of mass entertainment and there must never be too much of that?

Is it because she has lost her matching hat and her purse and her shoes and her dress that the kind old woman is weeping or because her adorable children have reported the dog's murder to the proper authorities thus convincing their blind mother who must now appear before a judge who is fat and greedy and will sentence her to death in light of the fact that the dog she most assuredly killed was not hers at all but belonged to the judge's father was in fact his mother who had run away to a life of decadence in Paris and returned transformed through some great feat as a German shepherd who sipped French champagne through a straw and danced until midnight with men of little character?

Was it really the kind old woman who never had a name because her father died at her birth and her mother before she was born and ever since then was referred to as a kind little old woman was it truly she who committed the offense or was it the man who sold her the indigo stick at the unheard-of price of 25 cents plus tax making a grand total of $46,983.45 which remains unpaid to this day for the man mysteriously disappeared in the night as thieves and loaves of wheat bread are apt to do and thus everything was made right according to every law but one which remains on the books though everyone dreads it for this is the custom of people these days and how can custom be challenged when even the dogs obey as they should because it is written some place in a faraway land that mongrels will obey the stupidest of customs or was it mongeese the Scripture mentioned in chapter 6 verse 44?

Who can the man possibly be in the black mask that allows only his eyes to peer out that is preparing to behead the kind old woman with a very large ax that he undoubtedly inherited from his drunken old father who once slept with a goat to see if there was a difference thus losing his organ and the respect of most men who had survived the experience as most of them do and was forced forever to wear a black mask and chop off old women's heads and after his death leave his son this great legacy who was a man of great strength and able to crack the strongest of neck bones though he hated the sight of blood for blood is a most unsettling substance and one in which the masked man once drowned a cat for no particular reason except the cat ate his birth certificate thus making him unborn which was as it should be because the man was a vile and evil creature who would chop off the heads of kind old women?

Will there be a reprieve from the governor from the judge from the dog from the cat from the 2,486 children from Igor or maybe the dirty old bum who now caresses the palm of the girl who sits crying by the bus stop because the bus has not come for almost two years and who was once said to be a statue because the pigeons had no qualms about landing on her head which always made her cry she hated the pigeons just as much as she hated the sun and the moon and the stars and winter and summer and Asia and Argentina and everything in between that reminded her that her mother was a peacock and her father was a fat and greedy potentate who ate pork chops for breakfast lunch and dinner until one day he grew a pig's tail and became a favorite with loose women?

Is it the children who will inherit the lost indigo stick or the man who was never paid for it or the law or the aristocrat whose wife was killed by it no matter how mistakenly by the kind old woman whose head was severed some time ago by the masked man for it has always been said by the wisest of men that those women who allow themselves to become old and kind no matter how innocently must be treated as shabbily as possible and finally be killed because they have committed the most wicked of sins and one which neither God nor man nor anything in between should can or will ever forgive and all this is true because fate has repeated itself many times over making an example of these transgressions just as Monday may never come twice in a week and Good Days never come at all and cabbages are eaten only by paupers who tell stories of elves that dance merrily in the rain and never have worries which allows them to live forever in ignorance and eating ice cream will make you happy and ambrosia is made from the tears of honeybees who are banished from their hives by an ungrateful queen and love is never as good as the idea and though this is factual facts can nauseate the strongest of stomachs and must never be taken before noon for this will cause cynicism in the most hopeful heart and well-ordered home as has been claimed repeatedly by the man in black trousers who pretends to be smiling at a painting by Bruegel but is actually gritting his teeth for he hates his small part in this exaggerated soap opera?

Did the kind old woman lose her head in much the same way she lost the indigo stick which is a meager inheritance for 2,486 adorable children can never be replaced no matter how hard the chief inspector might try for it is his job to make right such losses of valuable property especially for miserable orphans like these even the dog has disowned them on the advice of her lawyer who lives in a large white house on the banks of the Amazon which has 986 bathrooms and only one door through which many have passed their lives on the way to true justice or the toilet which is to say that the house is haunted by ghosts that haunt it day and night causing nearby villagers to become devout and superstitious and sacrifice their children to gods of antiquity who have long since died or moved away to other states making all the villagers' offerings useless ash and this will someday exterminate the villagers and all the world will mourn their passing and rob their graves and steal their culture and tell obscene stories about their mothers and finally turn them into myths that probably never existed and the Amazon will dry up like a droplet on a grill and no one will ever miss it?

harold mcneil robinson

ADODI EYES

HAROLD McNEIL ROBINSON attended Phillips Academy in Andover, Massachusetts, Saint Olaf College in Northfield, Minnesota, and San Francisco State University. He returned to his place of birth, Brooklyn, New York in 1983 after teaching and training in Minnesota, California, Saudi Arabia, and North Yemen. He is a past president and board co-chair of Gay Men of African Descent. He is currently an Associate Staff Analyst with the New York City Department of Mental Health, and is also a practicing massage therapist. His work has appeared in *The Pyramid Periodical*, *The National Association of Black and White Men Together Journal*, *Take Five Magazine*, *The People's Journal*, and *The Road Before Us*. He was a contributing guest editor for *Queer City*.

THE BRIDGE

My mind submerges
as my body stretches
over a river of sleep
across my bed
spanning gaps in time and place
creating power in the darkness
from one day to the next

People have died building bridges
above moving valleys
like the Hudson
green-dollar meadows of concrete
in Manhattan
Langston sang of rivers
I want to sing about bridges

Forged by fire to conform
with the land
arching skeletons of steel
in suspension
bend their backs by design
bring you to me
me to you

Drummers hit a wave-like pitch
above a musical stream
choruses wail at the joining
of two shores
safe passage out of bondage
beyond a beast
borne by rivers of blood
new way into a future
when we can freely lay our bodies down
support for all we know and love
but never forget
people have died building bridges

harold McNeil robinson

60

Maybe virginity had become too tiresome
adolescence too prolonged
the need to be with a man so great
random sex would be kept hidden
with no one to confide in
on the way to a secret date
there in the heartland
They were young
still boys in many ways
mostly poor and slight-framed
mostly Black
one from Laos
the police took him back
to a death not captured on videotape
by a mind that found sexual power
over unconscious bodies
cutting them up
eating corpses
Maybe they were too young
to sense the clues
his blank gray expression
his predatory cunning
the smell of blood
like a butcher's shop
a meat packing plant
dinner at Jeffrey Dahmer's

When I eat raw cashews
I'm boarding the bus from Mombasa
or waiting to embark
across the river to Malindi
At each crossing
vendors sell raw cashews
till we near the Somali border
One last ferry there to convey us
to the island port of Lamu
paradise in an archipelago
undisturbed by the engines of progress
far away from the chill of Nairobi

When I eat raw cashews
I think of you
slowly moving off the noisy guesthouse bed
silently onto the woven floor mat
My hand moves quickly
over your mouth
to muffle the clever cries
of a proverb in Swahili
telling how two African-Americans
in Kenya
became one
long
slow
embrace

harold McNeil robinson

I look on you with Adodi* eyes
I am with you even now
You look at me
You stay with me
and there is comfort
for you allow me my Adodi ways
Yes, this moment can last
as a lifetime in itself

So I bite your breast and ass
suckle your nipples
nuzzle your underarms
and crotch
though you resist and struggle
annoyed by the condoms
that finally vanish anyway
when no longer needed

My inner voice quakes and starts
at your touch
and when enough has no more meaning
or measure
I see in the fuzzy morning light
that you too see me with Adodi eyes

*Adodi: from the Yoruba, describing a person of transcendent sexuality called
to or chosen for a priestly or shamanic role; in the African-American context,
"in the life" or "one of the children."

NIGHT WATERING

For Edna Hong

No one sees me
so late at night
in reoccurring meditations
of movements
from an almost muscular memory
like kneading bread
or planting yams
as I tilt the watering can
over a deck of flowers
or hose vegetables
in garden darkness

Sounds so clear and liquid to me
true as night
more certain than fog
to penetrate a dry patch
of my neighbor's land
soaking deeply down
to cultivate unknown networks
of roots

Sometimes from my doorway
in full moonlight
I feel the even more
consoling downpouring
of shining droplets
raining on shoots and outcrops
of new growth

BRING IT ON HOME

Smoke from below
but no fire
I could not sleep
for fear of what might have come
with all the sirens

The thought of loss
numbed my heart
Your walk and talk
eased my soul
The hand that
warms my shoulder though
could bring up flames
that burn
              you know

TEARS BEFORE I KNOW YOU

For Roy and Tyrone

1.
So ready to be in love again
the care that time has taught
is not as skillful
at these acrobatic emotional feats
as one might like to be

Renovations have caused spiritual upheavals
All the mirrors are off the walls
I cannot be hynotized by my own image
but I can be by yours

Further restraint is not sublime
I need a mate
We come with past hurts
Old wounds that inhibit the desire

2.
Fear and need conspire
to distance us from
touching, talking, trusting too much
killing on cue with
acid-tongued punctual precision
or hot and honeyed untidiness
lip-synching to those around us
silently read
No space is safe
except for your therapist's or mine
Could we be more than
handsomely paired examples
of middle age and new class
What happens to the joy
and enthusiasm of early meetings
when two men undress each other
and begin to strip away
psychic layers with innocent desire
Does the price of such knowledge
grow so great
as to freeze all exchange and send us fleeing
like newly-freed men
from a slavish marketplace

3.
Our bodies' forced inflation
on stale and tainted air
now practice such economy
with our souls
The passing of each parcel
brings a tear
for it may only be
a token of what we can never know

You gotta be fast
Not cool to be slow
No time to explain
Just gotta have it
Use it,
Eat it up, consume
Get there, be there
In it, on it, over it
I'm right
Look, act, talk right
It's about me
You can't get close
I'm over, down
Like that speedy rabbit playboy
That New World cat
Don't chill now, hurry up
No, wait
You got
I need a token
Wanna be a token?

LE BÂTON D'OR

For Craig G. Harris

The gleam of
any sunlit day
warms that decorated vessel
as it moves in marathon
to end a century
proudly twirled so high
at the head of each parade
with vital messages
coded and ornate
inscribed names
memorable dates
passed from hand to hand
with no small effort
to those who would grasp
on its enduring way
across the great millenium

COCKTEASE

A tropical pose
     invites attention
Smiling eyes
     ignite affection
A boyish grin
     makes no demands
     gives no wet promises
     on holding hands
Could a casual desire
     to please
erect the profile
     of a cocktease

Bad boy, you stood me up
Bad boy, you say you don't know why
"I won't do it no more
Do you forgive me"
Bad boy, you said you'd make it up
But you messed up again
Were you out buying reefer
Or just drunk again
Bad boy, did you sleep it off
With another date
Did you ask him to teach you
To do the condom thing
Bad boy, I think you like *it rough*
Maybe that's why you're so bad
Should I slap you around
Should I throw you down
Would you give up some love
When Mr. Pain's in town
Your body's so smooth
Your buns are so firm
I can make us both feel good
Bad boy, see how you squirm
Bad boy, what's your limit
How far can we go
With much more disrespect
And heavier blows
I could send you out of this world
No, bad boy
Didn't come here for that
My time's too precious
To get caught up in a trap

LOVE AT A DISTANCE

For Wayne and Steven

1.
So hard to give the love you want
So high the price
if we should disappear
just not be there
as absentee parents or previous lovers
Our thoughts coincide for a moment
like trains running briefly
on parallel tracks
Powers that pressure
engineer our submission
sacrifice suicidal
of a sex out of vogue
subdued underground
by recycled morals

2.
Love at a distance
seems so religious
A Black gay Messiah might be
fun to run over
locomoting to freedom, glory, and gold
He had called my attention
to swollen lymph nodes
shaking my hand stiffly
when he knew I'd undress him
after months of reflection
Talk and touch were taboo
silence seemed such a friend
Love at a distance
was so safe and secure
No need for unblocking
reservoirs of emotion

3.
Passing subway lights flicker
Windows run in reverse, stand still
move forward like silent movie frames
None of the passing fluorescent faces
reminds me of you
My thoughts reel backward
to scenes of late summer
hotel crimes of passion near Rock Creek
our annual picnic, a visual feast
of tight buns, thighs, and dewy eyes
Nights of talking long distance
projecting our bodies across
four hundred miles of New England

4.
Love at a distance
may not know of our suffering or even care
Are you back in remission
The trains of love and thought
rock and rattle with a kind of inertia
that prevents any movement
Railroading into the future
across boundaries real and imagined
the frontiers of your thighs
or the seat of your mind
Railroading, railroading out of that time,
out of your love and into your like
Love at a distance
mourns for the losses, in patchwork
whistlestops, in remembrance
leaves only remnants of care and concern
from the need to be needed
and so loved in return

here to dare

PAULNESS

For Paul Thompkins

His grandpa taught him what counted
how to deal with folk
tally orders
for fruit and garden produce
off of acres of family land
In a homehouse undivided
with a constant of love
a locus of protection
his skills grew exponentially
to form a problem-solving way of life
He could calculate the shortest distance
from the heart to the brain
or measure love on a curve
like ancient architects
Even the pyramids of Egypt
were not safe
from the needle of his compass
With his given latitude of will
longitude of sight
he now dares to rule the world
from a Georgia classroom

Craig a. reynolds

I WONDER NOT WHY,
BUT WHEN . . .

Native Washingtonian, CRAIG A. REYNOLDS has read widely in D.C., Baltimore, New York City, and Boston. Reynolds' poetry has appeared in the anthologies: *In the Life, Brother to Brother*, and *The Road Before Us*. His writings have also appeared in *Brussel Sprouts, Changing Men, Turnstile, Lip Service, The Country Poet, Blacklight*, and other periodicals. A writer-editor, Reynolds is an officer in the Smithsonian African American Association, and he is program coordinator for the Smithsonian Institution Lesbian and Gay Issues committee.

Acknowledgments:
Some of these poems were published in *Pegasus, World's Word, Feelings, Black American Literature Forum, DEROS*, and *Now Magazine*.

The weather-faded wheels and arms are eerily
    still, as if this were the rainy off-season.
Like scar tissue, scales of rust have seized
    the screws and hinges, springs and cranks.
Once a swirl of laughter and smiles
    enrapturing even adults despite their reason,
the carnival is deserted, its fun house
    mirrors shattered by adolescent pranks.
Though shadows now show through
    my splintered planks,
I want my wheels to turn once more, my neon
    rainbows to burn,
and the marks to gawk at my tattooed lady's flanks.
I want to be the carny again where smart-aleck
    boys gladly lose all they've earn-
ed. So grunt my grimy plugs out,
    then grind and regap each in turn.
With those limber long loving fingers, fid-
dle my engines for their leanest burn.
    With eyes skyward yet stern,
let your arms plump as you pulley
    my floppy big top into a taut pyramid.

Then yank my starter cords with a hearty "hyup!"
and start me up. Oooh, daddy, please
    let's start right up.

Craig A. Reynolds

My craft skims so low that, from land, when I dawn
on the horizon, I seem to rise
       like Venus from the ocean's
abysmal plain. The slick outcrops
       and bird's-foot delta curl
in the sea, resembling sleep-tossed obsidian locks.
My shadow flutter-kisses
       the beach's noble brow. The domes
of the temple and government house appear closed eyes,
and the idle main streets perhaps
       the T of the nose and mouth.
Beyond the capital, two quiet volcanoes
thrust their dark craters above the flat terrain
where in the sun the sparse growth is translucent
as pubescent hairs, but from the hollow where I land
the thatched underbrush soon
       becomes the young trees
which, in turn, rise to the forest's
       crown canopy. The trees thin
as they climb the two mountain ranges which diverge
in the morn's receding mists like legs akimbo
under a coverlet I have lifted.
I begin my explorations.

I have a paunch I never could have had in the wild.
Rather than being enticed by the scent,
        I am disturbed
by the thud of two-week old cuts which taste
like campers' candles. True, there are
        no night-scoped rifles
behind boulders or in the planes,
        yet I want to stride with my pride
through chest-high wild grasses,
        I want to chase my meals,
to stalk those 60 miles-per-hour limbs
until grace and youth succumb to strength and guile.
You call this meat! You have not
        savored meat unless
you've been blinded by still-spurting blood,
        have ripped warm flesh from a struggling
thigh, and growling contentment,
        have sucked the creamy marrow from the bones.
Set me free, I want meat, I must kill, I will be free.

Half-listening to Bernstein's analysis
     of Barenboim's interpretation of Beethoven's
     "Thirty-Two Variations on a Theme by Diabelli,"
while lounging on a leather divan
     in a fiftieth-floor condo, I began
the interview by pointing to a silver-framed enlargement
     above the electric fireplace. "That African
photo is your most famous, is it not?"
     "The dried grass is finer than vermicelli,"
my blond hostess recalled. "The chief himself gathers
     many colors and weaves the grasses into a design
     which strengthens the span."
We both contemplated the print of the chief's
     earth and grass home. Beyond it,
     also in focus, the village women farm-
ed. My hostess continued, "Their hoes rise
     in unison as they call and respond
     with a planting song set by the chief as a charm.
Their chief is the poet, priest, prophet,
     prefect, and protector of their clan."

Photographs spilled from a portfolio between us;
     the floor teemed with brown-
chested men wielding machetes and playing guitars.
     "Aren't these photos like your famous African one!?!"
     I exclaimed. "Not in the least!"
she countered, "They were taken continents apart,
     and the compositions differ." Yet I was spellbound
by a photo of rain-forest fighters marching
     with their arms interlocked, singing
     "The fighter and the farmer are brothers."
As she expounded on appropriate f-stops,
     I remembered that these fighters become writers
     again once the latest skirmishes
     with the junta have ceased.
They always live with a guitar over one shoulder
     and a machete over the other.

SILENCIO *(IN THE AFTERMATH OF THE MEXICO CITY EARTHQUAKE, SEPTEMBER 1985)*

The order goes forth from the orange-helmeted herald
      atop the highest parapet of precarious rubble,
"Silencio." The clatter of chain saws
      cutting concrete, the grating
of shovels uncovering — rather than covering —
      limp-limbed death, the babel of eloquent
      journalists masked in days of stubble,
and the ratchet of their cameras
      filing their international reports —
      all clamor stops. We stand wildcat-still, waiting
to hear the weak whimper of life. Although
      the temple's tapestry has returned to threads
and the basilica's golden dome has burst
      like a child's bubble, as if still venerating
we listen with stethoscopes, for tapping, shifting,
      kicking — any signal of life. When
      the bloodhounds lower their heads,
we hush, *"Silencio!"* and from mortar's grip with pickax
      Caesarean release life's fugitives into our arms.
When rats and buzzards promenade in the boulevard
      like arrivistes, one word just barely said,
"Silencio," scatters them. As mounting aftershocks —
      or are they new convulsions!?! — spread alarm,
"Silencio!" bows our heads in a moment of silence,
      next calms us, and then helps us resume our rounds.
Sometimes the word re-echoes sepulchrally from between
      the twisted orthodontia and dragon's teeth
      of an oracular modern ruin, and we then believe
      someone else safe from harm.
After days of double shifts, just when we would die on
      a desert of despair, the rallying cry resounds,
"Silencio," then as if at an oasis, we quaff the cool
      water of hope that another has been found.

Craig A. Reynolds

I cannot tell you I know just how sick
      the treatment makes you,
sicker, you say, than the sickness itself.
I cannot tell you I know what it's like
      to be restless all night,
retching and wishing for sleep or for death.
I cannot tell you I know the latest
      experimental treatment will prove a cure,
or that I know how the gawking interns,
      hushed clusters of doctors, and
punctual injections harass you like hell.
I cannot tell you I know what it's like to have pains
as persistent as collection agencies.
I cannot give you a sound reason to live,
if you have none yourself.

I cannot tell you that a sunset you'd see
      just might seem
more uncommon than any you've seen,
or that the locusts and roses in blooming
      will sweeten the air
more than any you've smelled until now,
or a friend's phone call will surprise you with joy
that you've known only one time before.
I cannot tell you that death wouldn't be so
      much better than life
under the present conditions,
because I've not known death
and cannot tell you of the things I've not known.

Yet of what I have known and you also have known,
I can tell you I would choose life,
under almost any conditions.

GUMMICK

Your legs which outwitted me wherever my toddler's
feet would take me, now like underbrush in a storm,
twitch in pain beneath the bed covers.

Your arms which pushed me so high I nearly took flight,
now knotted to the bed rails like frazzled ropes,
struggle to keep you from the shark's maw of death.

Your lips which insisted I say "Granny,"
when my young muscles could only say "Gummick,"
now seem to gurgle "Gummick."

HIBAKUSHA

      my countrymen call me
a survivor of the American attacks
on Hiroshima and Nagasaki.
My neighbors who were flash-kilned into statues
were luckier in their deaths than I.
Others whose charred skin regrew as keloids,
rubbery layers as pink as the occupying forces,
in their deformity were luckier than I.
Unsinged, unmarked I, a survivor,
buried the dead, healed the sick, and talked
of rebuilding our homes and our shrines —
until afflicted by fatigue and nausea.
I awoke covered with purple freckles,
petechiae the doctors call them,
but survivors call it all the A-bomb disease.
I never know whether to comb
my hair for fear brushfuls
might come out. Yes, it grows
back, but after a month, a year,
the sickness starts again.
The children I carried then are stunted,
and I cannot, dare not, conceive more.
How long will this nuclear umbrella
shadow my life and the lives

of generations to come?
The typhoon that September swept
away the skeletons of bridges
and buildings, but what deluge
will raze the twisted superstructure
within my bones and cells?
A *hibakusha* can only wonder.
"*Hibakusha*," employers shrug
when they refuse to hire me.
"Trifling *hibakusha*," sneer my countrymen
surveying my "atomic slum."
"*Hibakusha!*" dismay affianced families
when they break engagements.
I hear, "*Hibakusha! hibakusha! hibakusha!*"
as if I had killed my brother.
For months I saw and smelled death;
the dead populate my dreams.
A *hibakusha*'s real countrymen are the dead,
for well, for awhile, or ill,
a *hibakusha* merely waits for death —
waits sleepy yet sleepless,
restless yet never alive.
"*Hibakusha*," my countrymen call me.
What do your countrymen call you?

Watch what you make of me,
clubfoot, when you beat me
on your raging forge.

When you thrust me into
your snaggletoothed furnace
with its red-lying tongues,

watch that you do not instead
whittle my whimpering
babe's fat away

and taunt my supple young
muscles into sinewy
high-tension cables.

When, with scorn, you spit
upon me, watch that your
sizzling spittle does not cure

the steel and ease it
across the whetting stone.

Watch that when you holler

"gook-nigger-spic-faggot-dyke-bitch"
your blasts do not cool the fevered steel

just enough for it to face
the fire once again.

Watch what you make of me.

REFLECTIONS (THOUGHTS ON MAYA LIN'S VIETNAM VETERANS' MEMORIAL)

It is a memorial wall but there is no old-world wailing,
rather the stifled sobbing of the living,
        ghostly pale reflections who search
in the depths of the black granite surface
among the pandemonium of 57,939
        machine-cut names of sailing,
flying, and marching dead.
        The mourners, finding the one —
        at most ten names — which means tears, first lurch
with bitter joy then gasped relief at this public token
        of their private grief. With their ker-
chiefs, they hide tears from their once-questing eyes
        and polish the comforting words they've found.
Upon this black screen, blurred images
        of mourners come and go, the silver ones
of the rebellious Washington and civil Lincoln stay,
        and jets pass to lands of which we've only read.

I climb an earthen embankment to stand at the vertex
        of the V-shaped wall — above the living
        and the dead—
and there reflect upon this funereal chevron.
        It is the somber stripe of the many PFC's
        whose blood nur-
tured that foreign ground; a V for the still living
        victims whose phantom limbs yet seem to pound,
and those who as wives, husbands, lovers, friends, parents,
        and orphans lost, not a part,
        but a whole beloved body to some
        children's riddling rounds;
a V for Vietnam, that conundrum which continues
        to confound us; a V-shaped graph of the intersection
now of living with dead, West with East, and past
        with a future in which chances indeed abound;
but, most of all, the V of winged victory,
        not of human over human, but of mind
        over napalm chaos. A victorious resurrection.

here to dare

TO A YOUNG WALKMAN WITH HEADPHONES

Seeing you, I know how mute our loved ones
feel when they try to talk with us
from beyond the grave.
I try to coax a smile from you
to cheer my day. You neither evade
my glance nor curl your lips in a curse.
It is worse; you are absorbed.
Does the world, my world of the dead,
hurt you more than your music hurts my ears?
Is that why that steel apparatus
embraces your head with poised pairs
of hypodermic pistons?
Teeming like a culture in a petri dish,
the din with which you inject yourself
makes you dance like you're showering at Auschwitz.
Is the music your firebreak against forest fires?
Does it forestall the fireball?
Or does that Berlin Wall of sound gulag
disturbances within the townships of your mind?
Does your catholic right hemisphere challenge
the protestant imperialism of your left?
Does the aching drum insist
you want your homeland back?

I have been death's detainee.
The insurgent and counterinsurgent death squads both
used my livestock and my family for target practice
and cleaned their superpower rifles with our butter.
Uniforms, only following orders,
tattooed a serial number on my soul.
The piece of rag they pinned on me
for identification became my flag.
Against the cattle prods, the water cannons,
          and the enemas of interrogation,
your painful cacophony provides puny defense.
I danced on the slave ship to the rhythm of the whip,
lived, and can show you how to survive
the revolutionaries' nerve gas and the authorities' batons, if

you lower your force-field of The Grateful Dead.
But to live we must talk, then we can chorus,
"Never again death; ever again life."

IN-SPECTRE

If I would let myself look I'd see the streetperson's head
apparently float in the steam above his makeshift stove.
He seems to leer at lab rats running a maze
        till they're dead,
but I scurry to work, a squirrel —
        neither my eyes nor mind rove —
fearing the stench of what he cooks
        might foul my Brooks Brothers clothes.
When I scamper at noontime to cover my margin
account at the broker's, the streetperson,
        at first, appears to doze,
yet as I pass him I fancy he jeers my latest bargain.
When I late-night at the law library to learn
        the skills of winning
by roting the precedents of corporate law,
the same streetperson sits superciliously grinning
as if he, such a failure, could discern any flaw.
In my nightmares, he refuses both welfare and shelter
but shares roast pigeon and his stiff clothes
        when I'm overwhelmed by the world's welter.

LET US BE EAGLES TOGETHER

I've languished in the steel and glass
bowels of this city and waited here —

for a beak to probe my breast's secret
down — waited for many-a-year,

for one whose mile-high shadow — and that
alone — would rout the grazers with fear.

That one has come; now let us go — from
the slaughter-bound who linger here,

from the nauseating circles of buzzards
who strut and scrap, pick and leer —

to gambol like Jacob and his angel
on yet loftier cloud-tiers,

to soar easily through rare cold-thinned
air, wings tip-to-tip and most sincere,

to hear the song of the solar wind as it
shears off our utmost sphere.

Let us be eagles together,
measuring the heavenly frontier;

let us preen, protect, provide for,
and hold each other forever dear.

Steve langley

SOMETHING TO BELIEVE IN

A singer, songwriter, and poet, STEVE LANGLEY has been featured in the award-winning Black gay film, *Tongues Untied*. His poetry has appeared in *The Road Before Us*, *Other Countries*, as well as other publications. His musical composition "In This Land" is the title song on an album by the internationally acclaimed Sweet Honey in the Rock. Several of his songs are being performed by Reverb, an a cappella group he sings with.

Acknowledgments:
Some of these poems were published in: *Black/Out*, *Other Countries*, as well as featured in the film, *Tongues Untied*.

When I was 10 years old, I asked
my mama while she was making potato salad:
"Mama, what's a homosexual?" She said:
      "It's a man who likes men."
"What's a lesbian?"
      "It's a woman who likes women."
"What makes them like that?"
      "I don't know, son. Nobody knows.
      It's a freak of nature."

When I was 14, I heard
her say to my stepfather:
      "We can't go nowhere
      without you winkin' and blinkin'
      and makin' advances at other men. I see you.
      I'll never trust you as long as you got
      a hole in your ass."

When I was 17, I sat
with my mother on our front porch
as she shriveled from cancer.
We watched the stars, felt the breeze
Tonight, I would tell her,
tell her that I was like the men
she told me about,
that I was like my stepfather...
Ants gathered the words at my feet.
I felt them rise through my toes, my ankles,
and my legs. They were creeping through me,
at my waist, in my stomach, my chest.
My throat got thick, my tongue heavy.
I needed to tell her what she already knew.
I began,

But I couldn't....

Steve langley

GROUND ZERO
(A NUCLEAR FAIRY TALE)

mama, li'l' sister, and i huddle under the covers
as missiles hurl from the earth.
we got ten minutes left.
i want to crawl under the bed while mama
takes her final pee but i remember that
my teacher says it is better to talk about
your fears.
mama returns
eyes sunk in her skull
forehead stuck out
mouth twisted round the side of her face.
she holds me in her skeleton arms.
she always understood.

WILDLIFE

were you an eagle, you would
swoop down on your victim
were you a cheetah, you would
spot the weakest among the herd
then sprint in for the kill
were you a shark, you would
smell blood and circle your prey
but the lamb in you keeps you at bay
still the hunger will not dissipate
fearing the consequence of vulnerable eyes
you keep your head bowed
grazing

BORROW THINGS FROM THE UNIVERSE

When you find yourself comin' up short
Borrow things from the universe
Take a little from the shelf
Grab some extra for yourself
It's all yours, go ahead
What's the matter, are you scared
Lean slightly forward on your toes
Point your chin toward the sun
Reach for distant galaxies
Peep over horizons
Can't you see
Win or lose you pay your dues
For latent fantasies
So first, reach, pull, grab
And snatch what's yours
From the universe

BEFORE THE LECTURE

two white students discuss the
significance of washington and jefferson
i hold yellow pages together with
a rubber band, binding so
fragile the musty paperback breaks
into chunks like clay tablets
"what are you reading?" one asks.
"the autobiography of malcolm x," i say
"oh, we're not familiar with that," the other sighs
eyes floating out of the window

Steve langley

BASIC TRAINING
(TO BE PERFORMED DURING PUSH-UPS)

Skyscrapers	Joy Sticks
Uh	Uh
Rods	Bats
Uh	Uh
Cylinders	Pens
Uh	Uh
Fishing Poles	Pencils
Uh	Uh
Flag Poles	Candles
Uh	Uh
Hoses	Microphones
Uh	Uh
Pipes	Arrows
Uh	Uh
Sausages	Guns
Uh	Uh
Hot Dogs	Bullets
Uh	Uh
Half Smokes	Torpedoes
Uh	Uh
Knockwursts	Missiles
Uh	UUUHHH
Bananas	
Uh	
Pickles	
Uh	
Cucumbers	
Uh	
Broomsticks	
Uh	
Dip Sticks	
Uh	
Stick Shifts	
Uh	

here to d*are*

Build a wall
I'll find a way to get over
Deal me a bad hand
Watch me change my luck
Turn up the heat
And I'll make it colder
Do what you want
I'm never giving up

THE ARTIST

all over this city
i hurl buckets of
red yellow blue
orange purple green
undaunted by the possibility
that i am spreading myself
too thin, i press on
i keep tossing colors against
bleak brick walls, hoping
something will endure
these harsh elements

WARNING

beware
of a writer
with delicate
sensitivities
for all your
intimacies
may end up on
a yellow legal pad

COMPANY

i see stains
on your sheets
and tell myself
it's chicken grease

i'm chocolate candy
a handful of cookies
the goodies you're forbidden
to eat
i'm a piece of cake
a slice of pie
an ice-cream bar
that chills your teeth
think of me
as your favorite treat
a pan of popcorn kernels
waitin' for the heat

THE PET SHOP

i
convert dollars to coins
and enter the labyrinth of lust
blue corridor leads to
dead space/no exit
hands become maps
cats backed against the wall
mice sniffing corners
a carnal chase in a stained maze
of disinfected funk
once inside the room, no telling
who'll devour whom
i am to be played
like a game-type thing
we are all lost
but some find their way
sooner than others

SOMETHING TO BELIEVE IN

Every time you turn around, he's chasing something
Baptized American, he's trying to make it any way he can
Shifting winds and changing times
Anybody can have a change of mind
But will he ever follow through
When will he achieve what he set out to do

No one, no one understands what sends him
Through these changes
So much, so much potential
Why is he so aimless

He's just reaching for something
Something to believe in
He's just reaching for someone
Someone who'll believe in him

Every time you turn around, he's moving somewhere
Sure did shake his family tree
Packed his bags and moved to the big city
Reeling from the desperate crowd
Hitchhiked till he found a safe midwestern town
Restless and misunderstood
Dreams of how he'll make it big in Hollywood

Every time you turn around, he's made a vow
He'll make it happen, everything will work out
Every time you turn around, he's made a vow
He'll make it happen, he'll make it somehow

He's just reaching for something
Something to believe in
He's just reaching for someone
Someone who'll believe in him

REVOLUTIONARY CREATURES

We know
More than we think we know
Poised yet unsure
But like nocturnal creatures
Our instincts will tell us
When it's
Time

CHECKLIST

Say yes to love
Say no to sex
Say you, say me
Oh say can you see
We are afraid of each other
Say sister, say brother
Are you still messin' 'round
Do you have a steady lover
Are you waitin' for the cure
Are you sure
Are you savin' yourself
Are you lovin' yourself
Have you come yet
Are your dreams wet
Is your sex safe
Is it already too late?

EXIT

Because you know the answer all too well
You dare not ask to stay
So you lie there, eyes gathering
Your things in half-light
Admiring the back of the stranger who
Faces the wall

Caressing the cool face of your watch
With a thumb, you play dumb
Pretending you're too naive to read
Body language

CEREESE

fired
'cause she wouldn't stay
in her place
one fiancé was gay
another married her best friend
on her wedding day
now music's her man
she croons the blues
sucks ice from a sloe gin fizz
and cackles before the punch line
somebody put another quarter
in the jukebox
and freshen the girl's drink

Black child, white child
Playing in the sand
Black child, white child
Hold each other's hand

Black mom, white mom
Wait a little while
Black mom, white mom
Forcing half a smile

Black youth, white youth
Taught to separate
Black youth, white youth
Now they learn to hate

Black man, white man
Working every day
Black man, white man
One gets better pay

Black folks, white folks
Walking with their canes
Black folks, white folks
Becoming the same

Black corpse, white corpse
See them lowered down
Black corpse, white corpse
Equal in the ground

Have you been to where the river's deep
Tested the waters with your toes
Have you waded in a gentle stream
Have you followed where it flows
Do you wish you had the wings of a bird
So you could take to the sky
Ever been up to a mountaintop
So you could see the other side

Some people spend their days
Dreaming about such things
Others go out and do
Tell me, what about you
Have you really lived, have you been here?
Have you really lived, have you been here?

Have you ever tasted honey sweet
Have you ever smelled a rose
Ever felt the wind against your cheek
Do you know what makes it blow
Have you ever seen a baby being born
Ever heard that first cry
Ever seen those first awkward steps
Fall and give it one more try

Some people spend their days
Dreaming about such things
Others go out and do
Tell me, what about you
Have you really lived, have you been here?
Have you really lived, have you been here?

Cary alan johnson

SURRENDER

CARY ALAN JOHNSON is an author, Africanist, and human rights activist. Originally from Brooklyn, Johnson has lived and traveled throughout Africa, Europe, and North America.

For Edward Caesar Nash, in love and friendship.

Acknowledgments:
Some of these poems were published in: *Other Countries, Outlook, Changing Men, Northlands, The James White Review, Queer City, Agni,* and *On Men and Intimacy.*

I remember being young feeling grown
at seven among the feet of many mothers
impatient with wallpapered kitchen
conversations and hot combs.

Twice-a-year she came
with the harvested suns of a thousand
Dixie streets
a visitor to Troy
bearing pecans for the women of our clan
who killed chickens and cooked pork in offering.

Our tribe is matri-local endogamous complex.
We trace our history from a common female deity.

Twice-a-year she came
bringing news from home
South
our harvest home
our burial home
our home in times of war and famine
South
we sent our sisters
pregnant with shame in love
South.

Twice-a-year she came
elders delayed decisions to her arrival
marriages births lives hung pending
we were ellipses to her exclamation
she judged wisely
she was the ballast of our family ship.

She taught us
that there is no shame in being poor
nothing white about being smart
no hope without forgiveness.

And when at twenty-two I returned
to Rocky Mount
and found her babbling vacant
mind broken and scattered in flowerpots
that schoolteacher intellect
now lining the pockets
of a torn housedress
I pointed my car toward Washington
and escaped
before the sun could set
on the blue tips of rigid mountains.
Those selfsame mountains she had crossed
twice-a-year
Christmas to New Year's
moverin' moverin'
Memorial to Labor
moverin' moverin'
going north
going Greyhound
bearing pecans
bearing wisdom
bearing love.

IRT

homeless woman on the train
shopping bag full of pain
pinned to her lapel, a button
she loves new york

BRIDGEHAMPTON

This ain't no place
for a Black man
to be from
this southern town
transplanted Wall Street
new rain rituals.
When is the moonlight
dancing?

Every summer
the acrid cut
of freshly tinged
lawns greeted us
the steel teeth
of Granddaddy's tractor
ate the winter wheat
and delivered
friendly worms for us
to multiply.

On the vista
the coo of waves
the roar of tanning
this Long Island sound
of burning....

STONED

I used your letter to roll a joint
and as your lies burned
I inhaled them;
they made me laugh.

Jelan and Jamali.
They born Lamu.
Grow together from boyness.
Grow together are one.
Together race seabirds. Share
cassava cooked in a blackened pot.

Jelan and Jamali.
Two sailors of a Lamu dhow.
Fish boat sail on water.
Jelan brown
high tones slim
long fine like rope.
Jamali is Swahili dark
warm shiny like
tanned blackness
muscles round like
knotted
rope.

Twenty-three.
Pay down on boat.
When they work they
sail.
Wazungu pay money
to ride on Jelan
and Jamali's boat.
Men women
pay money to ride the waves
of Jamali and Jelan.
Jelan long fine like sisal
like rope. They love
cassava cooked in a blackened pot.

When there is no work they
sail
and race seabirds.
Smoke laugh dance on water.
Tell tales of Lamu fishermen.
Sleep on bottom of boat.
Sleep on sail as mattress.
Sleep on coils and coils
of rope.
Each dreaming in his brother's arms.
And this is an African love poem.

SURRENDER

Last night
I fell silently into your
black sea.
Hair everywhere, in my
mouth, deep inside me,
deep, deeper
than we'd ever
gone before.
Did you know this
time would come?

If there is a wind
let it blow
here now
let it burst with salt
froth and
foam
let it whip
round mountains
till mountains
rain.

My forefather
was chief
of a village by the sea.
He rode the wind
with warriors
talked with fishes —
a Great Fish was his god.

There it is.
Catch it.
This wind flies up
and sparks me.
My eyes to the west
a Great Fish is in the sky.
Words of water are calling me home.

THE PIERCING

A biker did the trick
white snow-
addicted angelic
placed one rough hand
(fresh from the grip of his Harley)
onto my brown biceps
squeezed me man-hard
as he guided the steel needle
through my nipple
rigid in the bite of forceps.
"You okay, baby?"
That was no question.

My lover looked on
oh so
aware of this surgical subtext
fucking with instruments
thrilled at the vision
of my tongue
thick and spit-heavy
shining the boots of Jimmy Dean.
Was this the ménage of which we'd spoken?

The pain was like lightning
when he entered me.
The violence of his caress
split me like a tree
severed in the fury of an April storm.
(I remained hard for days).

Now this ring this circle jerk.

This must be faggot alchemy.
He instructs as wizard to apprentice:
        Flesh turns silver to gold.
        Blood keeps silver sterling and true.
        The yin. The yang.

In his grip
I am a teenager again
innocent and pure
strapped to a rack at the Mineshaft
one naked bulb-lit night.
A simple time
before all my dreams came true
and I woke up
rich blond meteoric.

In an antique porcelain tub I lay
ready for harness for bridle for riding
crop
ferocious id snarls unleashed
pitbulls sensing this bitch's heat
nazis, bikers.

He instructs as wizard to apprenticeship:
        Each night with purest of cotton — ablution.
        Each night when the moon rings high — rotation.
        The yin. The yang.

In this way I
was healed
became holy
grew a third eye
come to testify....

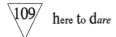

PROTECTION
For Jay at the big Three-0

You cruise Harlem
wave your masculinity
a white flag
in the face
of disbelief

no surrender.

The gym gets
all your time
as if eating weight
will abate your
fear of thinning

hair is a blessing
at thirty
yours is close thick
black
mine never touched
beyond the boundary
of disappearance.

At thirty
you overcame
came into your own
way of being
now
I find you
suddenly
breathtaking.

Harlem boys you say
are more sophisticated
than Brooklyn's
I wonder
if sophistication is what
you're after.

Cary alan johnson

You say we're all in this together.
But some of us don't know
that forty isn't promised
nor thirty-one.

Wear it for *me*, I say
and dress you up
in plastic
at thirty
none of us is free
no one of us is free
not to know.

NANNIE

They shall come to live with us
my grandparents,
their ghosts hang dripping from December bones
like Monday's wash, Wednesday's wash, Friday's...
The stench will not leave but lingers
in the hairs of my grandfather's nose.

I turned away from you
in your antiseptic get-well bed
mother of my mother.
Holding yourself together with bits of twine
a yellowed piece of seam
binding torn desparately from
a dress you wore to church.

I have your height, they say
my father's nose
my mother's worry
your endless desire to be with God,
to be eternal light.

One
is not enough.
Never was
mine a life
of finding strength
in numbers.

Too
often when we
flipped the coin
to decide who
would do who
I came up short.
Tails
I lost.
You took me
through changes
'cause I refused to ride
bareback
like the other troopers
on this mission.

Three
tubes enter you
fire water earth
no air you
breathe stop
breathe stop.
"Pull it down,"
you scrawl on a pad
no longer able to speak.
My dick comes instantly to life
"Pull it down,"
and I remove my mask
praying the strings of my life
the breath of this living

Cary Alan Johnson

won't rush the next step
of a journey begun
with a single nut.

Four
days later
at the hospital
your bed a calm white sea
stretches forever and ever
over the tallest trees
in Fort Greene Park.

Five
years was a long time to love.
I could've bought a house
finished grad school
wrote several plays
made amends with my brother
instead I bought flowers
and watched them die
again.

Six
close friends have stepped out on blind faith.
Seven
if you count my cousin lingering at D.C. General.
Today I make use of free time
map lines on my body
catalog true bruises
occasionally dream of love
with a gone man
a yesterday man
a numbered man.
Sometimes it feels like
we are all numbered men.

here to dare

CHANGING MEN
For Franklin Abbott

living life
in the cracks that things
fall through
dark has never
known this color
this hue
this total
void

time falls off
a man's life
and he is left wondering
am i a job
a wife
a children

am i nothing
do i nothing
is my singleness a punishment
was my coupling the crime

time falls off
a man's head
and he is left
bald shining
what wise wide thoughts
what wisdom
does it hold
that I cannot see
this man's head
these many years
this single radiant life

david Warren frechette

TOO THROUGH

DAVID WARREN FRECHETTE was a prominent journalist who died on May 11, 1991, of AIDS-related complications. His essays, reviews, and interviews appeared in *The City Sun, Penthouse, New York Native, The Advocate, Essence, The Amsterdam News, Black Film Review,* and *Gentlemen's Quarterly* . His poems and short stories have been published in *RFD, In Your Face, The Pyramid Periodical, Out/Look,* and the anthologies *Brother to Brother* and *The Road Before Us.* He was actively involved in the organizations Men of All Colors Together/New York, Gay Men of African Descent, Gay Males S/M Activists, and Other Countries.

Acknowledgments:
Some of these poems were published in: *The Pyramid Periodical, Brother to Brother, Queer City, RFD,* and *In Your Face.*

Once again,
Your mouth has written a check that
Your ass can't cash.

Once again,
You are not with me
When you said you would be.
And when confronted tell
Tales that would shame Scheherazade.

Once too often,
You've stood me up without warning,
Turning our few good times together into
Colorful ingredients in a recipe
For inconsistency.

If lies caused tooth decay,
You'd have a mouthful of dentures.
Your friendship's much too expensive,
And a more cost-effective model of you
Has got to be on the horizon.

Lust, masochism, and self-deceit
Bound me to you like a fly in a spider's web.
Reps of sugar-coated raps
You copped from Black ghetto neighborhoods
You grew up in,
Snared me in a net of hallucinatory charm,
Persuading me to believe your
Every other word.

With a suitcase of carefully selected jive,
You've bullshitted your way
Through bosses, beaus, two sets of parents,
And all but the sturdiest of pals.

Rest homes around the nation are full
Of men prematurely aged, waiting for you
To shuck your boyish charm and get real.

You can pack up your wardrobe of threadbare,
Insincere, and sorry excuses then victimize
Some brand-new fool with them.
You are traveling my mind's highway
On your way to oblivion, and brother,
It's all downhill on foot.

God help me to commit certain warning signals
To memory, like the alphabet and the lyrics to
Lady Day's greatest hits.

I shall limit my dealings with anyone under 25
To pats on the back, handshakes,
And handsomely paid campus lectures.
If they tell me they find me attractive,
I'll tell them they're either looking for
A father figure or they've found a new drug
That is clouding their judgment.

I shall forever loathe the sight of black
Velcro sneakers, plucked brows, tattooed limbs.
I shall distrust anyone who has a part-time job
And still no money to spend on
Their damned selves when we go out.

And I shall curse the state of New Jersey
For having to trek across state lines
To find the same heartaches available
Within New York's five boroughs.
No more meetings across the river to be
Blinded by the lights of Jungleland.

here to dare

Combing back streets and badlands in
The spirit of the night,
Racing through unfamiliar scenes,
Dancing in the dark in search of
Your replacement should prove a Herculean task
Which I intend to attack *con gusto*
And enjoy to the max.

You have not been a totally worthless adventure.
You have inspired poetry in spite of yourself.
Think of this poem neither as a fond
Nor bitter farewell but as a process server
Who has just handed you your walking papers.

SAFE HARBOR

Though destiny did not decree
That we become lovers,
It's in your arms I find
Safe harbor from
A tidal wave of woes
Threatening to engulf me.

Your smiling eyes are my lighthouse.
Your lips seal out chaos.
The smoothness and warmth of your body
Keeps the coarse chill of
The everyday world at bay.
And I'm not afraid to christen you
My temporary shelter from the storm.

It's summer and
Every other mother's son
Struts the steam-drenched asphalt
Like ripe walking fruits
And gourmet treats with torsos...
Wantonly stalking your divided attentions,
Boosting the temperature easily
Past the one-hundred degree mark.

Summer is a drop-dead gorgeous Black man
With the height of the Watusi and
The profile of Renauld White.
Faces that bear witness to
The influences of Africa, the Caribbean,
And nearly forgotten Native American tribes.
Tongues that testify in a polyglot of accents
From Dresden-like ghettos to Ivy League dorms.
Chocolates so sweet, fine, and delectable
That the Swiss would be truly jealous.
Strong brows set in tandem
With piercing wise eyes.
Black, brown, and beige skins all glistening
With the glow of good nutrition
And the limitless promise of ecstasy
To conquerors who can triumph over attitude
In the quest of their selected prizes.

Summer is a Dolph Lundgren-type blond
With chiseled features and cornsilk hair
Strolling beside you in Technicolor jams,
Which all but hide
Prime-cut bone-crusher calves.

Summer is a bad-ass Hispanic *hermano*
Anywhere from sixteen to fifty,
Collars casually open
To reveal sun-tanned chests.
Street dudes with mouth-watering
Cuelos and *bichos* oven-stuffed into
Shape-clinging slacks their sisters
Would find too restrictive.
Summer is a middle-class Nuyorican too,
Emitting Errol Flynn effects
In Armani threads,
Concealed sensuality seeping
Through his garments.
You want to kiss their ambivalent eyes,
Grip their uptight fists
As you take them down,
Jam your tongue against theirs
In an invasive maneuver
Worthy of a Green Beret,
As their surrendered machismo
Shatters in a burst of cries and whispers.

Summer is a leather/denim cowboy
Of any color, make or model you choose,
Striding deliberately between J's,
The Spike, and The Eagle until your eyes lock.

Everywhere you go and
Any which way you turn,
The streets teem with men who populate
Your most torrid fantasies,
Stoke the fiery furnace
Of your imagination,
And even insist on stowing away
In your daydreams.

In these all-too-somber plague-scare days
Lust is the howling animal within us
That refuses to die a coward's death so...
We whistle with our eyes and subtly
Wet our lips in anticipation
Of passionate dream scenes
With broad-shouldered,
sun-baked construction hunks,
Fickle youths with swimmers' builds,
Flint-eyed poets, and chunky truckers,
All of whom seem self-designed for
Our lust-ridden perusal and the
Satisfaction of our most riveting desires.

DIAGNOSIS

I know the reason your moods
Have waxed hyper-mercurial lately.
Why, you've been so beastly, the zoo
Has reserved a cage in your name.

Testing *HIV*+ has thrown your life
Into a pessimistic tailspin.
You feel everything's over —
Save for the final shout.

Although I know you're not
The sentimental type
(No tears in the end and all that),
Regardless, rely on my support.

I'm sick of your hectic schedule
Shielding you from romantic commitment.
I'm bored beyond tears from
Having to beg to see you.
I'm tired of being the last one
In line for your love and affection.
And I've nearly gone blind trying
To see things your way.

When we first met,
Strauss waltzes played in the background
And Dietrich sang "*La Vie En Rose*"
In the distance.
Now Ashford and Simpson's fantasies have
Displaced Nona Hendryx, demanding
To know "Why Should I Cry?"
I've become a victim of the very tunes
Sung by Randy Crawford and Joan Armatrading.

You claim you love and miss me
Yet it takes you weeks to return my calls.
Your actions belie your language.
Our romance seems stricken with cellular anemia.
You kept me on standby during the entire
Holiday season, claiming you wanted
To see me but never saying when.

david Warren frechette 122

Let me not hesitate to thank you for
The anger and anxiety
You gave me for Christmas,
Or the loneliness and despair with which
I rang in the New Year.
I could find no counter to return
Such priceless gifts except for the
Well-worn ears of friends and acquaintances.
I wanted to swear out an arrest warrant
Against the spirit of St. Nick and chase
Yuletide carolers into the next county
With harsh, sad Robert Johnson blues.

You're a principal without principles and
If there were a court of love,
You'd be convicted of perpetrating a fraud
With malice aforethought.
Your previous boyfriend must have died
From emotional neglect, and I can't see
Myself suffering the same bitter fate.
I'd like to talk about your sorry ass
On Oprah's and dish you
Before millions nationwide.

If only I had kept you restricted
To the status of freeze-dried fuck-buddy
(Jump it, pump it, thump it, and dump it),
If I had donned my armor sooner,
This wounded heart would have taken
Far less time to heal.

Instead I chose to believe your
Giorgio-scented terms of endearment
("You're everything I've been looking for")
And I am now all the more betrayed
For having done so.

I'm not even about to pretend
That I don't miss my forty-plus
Butterscotch prince with your
Runner's legs and leonine smirk,
Or that winter won't be three times
As cold without you no matter
How many blankets and scarves I use,
Or that I couldn't ignite whole forests
With the torch I'll always carry for you.

You'll probably hunt down
Some Buppie you deem more your equal,
Someone to whom you can profess *amour*
Sincerely beyond the confines
Of your bedroom walls.
Saying goodbye to you has proven difficult,
So long to your memory downright impossible.
But just to show an absence of hard feelings,
Good luck with your next victim.

Do what your doctor dictates.
Listen to what nutritionists suggest.
Sacrifice hard-earned ducats to
The neighborhood spa.

Make minor-league investments in
A whole new wardrobe. Beware
Of any long-term plans and pray bi-
Monthly for a better class of boyfriend.

Saunter through quick-fix cruise areas —
Safer sex on the left mind speaker,
James Brown on the other —
Will you shed your guilty secret?

In a classic '40s gangster flick,
Bogart (or was it John Derek),
Advised, "Live fast, die young,
And leave a good-looking corpse."

The first is a fait accompli.
The second, biologically unfeasible.
And the third you're working on daily.
Two out of three in any game ain't bad.

THE THRUST OF THRUSH

Nutritionists will tell you: "Oh honey, you can eat
Cheese, butter, and pasta, in moderation please,
Just rinse your mouth with water inside out afterwards."
Try telling that to my thrush and see if it doesn't laugh.

No sugar, no vinegar — so long mashed potatoes!
No spice or ketchup — there go my beloved burgers!
No bread, no flour — so long blue corn chips!
No yogurt or liquor — there go my glorious pecan pies!

The list of accessible foods gets slimmer every hour.
Health stores help you out if the staff's not too spacy.
Thrush taught me AIDS is no joke, but I'm determined
To fight with the meager 100 pounds at my disposal.

THE REAL DEAL

Don't want death to catch me crying and acting like
        I been bad.
Don't want no hypocrites around my bedside making
        me feel sad.

When my man comes my way with His golden book and
        silver scythe,
Then says, "Come along now, David... it's the end
        of your life!"

I'll answer Him, "I'm a natural fighter, I ain't gonna
        go easy,
Although my breath is short, and my stomach is
        quite queasy."

If I must leave this world hunched over, I got this
        reliance
That death will have to find me, arms folded in
        defiance.

david Warren frechette   126

NON, JE NE REGRETTE RIEN

For Keith Barrow and Larry McKeithan

> *I had big fun if I don't get well no more.*
> — *"Going Down Slow"*
> *as sung by Bobby "Blue" Bland*

Sister Chitlin', Brother Neck Bone and
Several of their oxymoron minions
Circle round my sickroom,
Swathed in paper surgical gowns,

Brandishing crosses, clutching Bibles,
(God, *please* don't let them sing hymns),
Pestering me to recant the
Wicked ways that brought me here.

"Renounce your sins and return to Jesus!"
Shouts one of the zealous flock.
"The truth is I never left Him,"
I reply with a fingersnap.
"Don't you wish you'd chosen a *normal* lifestyle?"
"Sister, for *me*, I'm *sure* I did."

Let the congregation work overtime
For my eleventh-hour conversion.
Their futile efforts fortify
My unrepentant resolve.

Though my body be racked by
Capricious pains and fevers,
I'm not even *about* to yield to
Fashionable gay Black temptation.

Mother Piaf's second greatest hit title
Is taped to the inside of my brain
And silently repeated like a mantra:
"*Non, Je Ne Regrette Rien.*"

I don't regret the hot Latino boxer
I made love to on Riverside Drive
Prior to a Washington march.
I don't regret wild Jersey nights
Spent in the arms of conflicted satyrs;
I don't regret late-night and early a.m.
Encounters with world-class insatiables.

My only regrets are being ill,
Bedridden and having no boyfriend
To pray over me.
And that now I'll never see Europe
Or my African homeland except
In photos in a book or magazine.

Engrave on my tombstone:
"Here sleeps a *happy* Black faggot
Who lived to love and died
With no guilt."

No, I regret nothing
Of the gay life I've led and
There's no way in Heaven or Hell
I'll let anyone make me.

don Charles

RINGS ON GLOVED FINGERS

DON CHARLES was born thirty-two years ago in Kansas City, Missouri, where he still lives and works. "Writing and calligraphy give me the means to defy society's attempts to classify me as just another uneducated, unskilled, frequently unemployed Black man."

To LBJ, who made me write "An Open Letter To Black Men."

Got a brand new dance
from Howard Beach
and Forsythe County
that I wanna teach

It's for Black folks only
and it's rocking the nation
Get ready to groove
on a stone sensation

Well I saw you do The Monkey
and I know you can Twist
Here's The 'Way Back Walk
and you do it like this

Put your knees together
Let your arms hang down
Now stoop your shoulders
and shuffle around

Now stop good God
Do you hear me talking
Well you better get ready
'cause we're gonna start walking

Step 'way back
and clap your hands
for Tawana Brawley
and the Ku Klux Klan
Step 'way back
and pat your feet
for Michael Stewart
just work that beat

Step 'way back
and shake a tailfeather
for Eleanor Bumpurs
Let's do it together
Now step 'way back
Just one more time
for Willie Darden
and you're looking real fine

Now drop to the ground
like you're shot full of lead
Now scream
like a mob is stomping your head

Now back on your feet
but we're not at the end
Gonna start this dance
all over again

It's The 'Way Back Walk
People give it a chance
America wants you
to learn this dance

It's better than The Limbo
and The Cuban Slide
Let's boogie to the music
of Genocide

here to dare

Dear boy,
please be careful as you walk home alone.

Rings on gloved fingers,
rings in both ears.
Beauty-salon curls rising high
on your Audrey Hepburn head.
When you ride the bus alone at night,
please be careful as you walk home.

I know you see them
at the back of the bus.
I know you hear them!
B-boys, jeering
and leering at you.

Talking about kicking your ass!
Talking about drawing your blood!
Hard fists,
broken bones,
bloody curls.
Please be careful as you walk home alone,
dear boy.

Rings on gloved fingers,
rings in both ears.
Beauty-salon curls rising high,
princely,
and proud.

Too beautiful to die.

They call me the trash collector.
I collect cultural trash.
You know, ideas that used to be hip,
but ain't hip no more.
Shit like disco music,
platform shoes,
Cleopatra Jones movies,
and cake-cutter combs.

You know what they do with cultural trash?
They load it up on a boat
and take it 'way out on the ocean.
Then they dump it over the side.
But the trash collector,
he don't miss no tricks.
I'm always there
to catch it in a net when it falls.
Then I take the shit home,
and I store it in a shoe box
on the top shelf of my bedroom closet.

You know what I'm gonna do someday?
I'm gonna lay the pieces of cultural trash
end-to-end.
And I'm gonna tie the pieces together,
make me a real long rope.
Then I'm gonna come over to your house,
and strangle you with it.

There's a party in my pants
and I sure would be delighted
if you could come inside and dance.
You're officially invited.
Come safari in my jungle.
You can swing upon the vine.
Let me take you for a tumble.
How about a little wine?
Now as a rule,
I'm a humping fool,
and I don't wonder why.
Don't mean to be crass,
but I love a tight ass!
I'm just a horny guy.
I partied hardy all last week
in Memphis, Tennessee.
I didn't *hardly* reach my peak.
Now that's virility!
I've bumped and humped across the miles
from Maine to California.
I left behind contented smiles,
but, baby, let me warn you
that just one man
is not my plan!
I like to spread my seeds.
I party tough,
and I've got enough
to satisfy their needs.
You can't go wrong
with what I've got.
It's tops on every list.
So big! So long!
So wicked hot!
Come try you some of this.
There's room for you inside my pants,
and I'd be so excited
to have you come and take a chance.
Consider yourself invited.

don *Charles*   134

The filet mignon was excellent,
and the caviar was divine.
Then for the coup de grâce,
the host brought out his priceless jade decanter
filled with promises of love.
Trembling with delight,
the guest held her goblet before her,
and watched in mounting anticipation
as his sparkling syllables rose slowly to the brim.
He made an appropriate toast,
and she drank deeply of his passion.
But the guest found the flavor deceitful,
and with a cry of disgust,
she let her goblet fall to the floor.
As his false love spilled from the container,
and his dark lies stained the carpet,
she took her leave of him without a word.
What was there to say?
The filet mignon had certainly been excellent,
and the caviar had indeed been divine.
But the host had been so tasteless
as to serve love of a bad vintage.
So naturally,
the evening was spoiled.

Bette Davis stares wide-eyed
from the poster on the wall, stage right.
She has left the bright lights of the movie set
to come and live with us
where the light is dim,
and there are no cameras...
But here, the scenery is authentic.

He and I share this room.
The air is heavy,
and we breathe cautiously.
Bette can sense the tension between us.
She sees the hateful faces I make at him
behind his back;
she hears the nasty things he says about me
when I am away.

She could break the tension
with a classic catty remark.
But with her mocking smile,
and a cigarette
balanced loosely between her fingers,
she merely observes
as we play out our little melodrama.

She knows the lines so well.
She recognizes
the sarcasm with which we speak them.
We recreate roles she has already played.
And she knows it won't be long now
until "the bitch" enters the scene
and steals it.

don Charles

"Hey, Mr. Shopkeeper! What's the deal?
This bullshit just can't be for real!
No sooner am I in the door,
you're trailing me around your store
and watching everything I do!
Does my color bother you?"

Yesterday, I went downtown
to stock up on some things.
I stopped in at the grocery store
and bought some chicken wings.

But when I headed for the door,
I had this confrontation.
The manager, he grabbed my arm
and made an accusation.

The bastard yanked my arm so hard,
it nearly left the socket!
He claimed I stole some candy bars
and stuffed 'em in my pocket.

"I oughta call the cops!" he yelled.
I said: "Why don't you, then?"
He hollered: "They'll arrest you
if you come in here again!"

I told him: "I don't shop in stores
where Black folks get harassed!"
You wanna know what I did then?
I showed my BIG BLACK ASS.

People, hear some good advice —
don't let me have to tell you twice!
The color of respect is green.
Don't spend it where they treat you mean.

I hate you as much as I love you, Black man.

Back in grade school,
you called me:
"Sissy!"
"Pussy!"
"Punk!"
By the time I got to junior high,
you added:
"Fag!"

And I will never forget
how you terrorized me.
No, I can never forget
how you ridiculed me.
All you ever gave me was a hard time.
You only cared enough to put me down.

I called you my father,
and you stood me up time after time.
I called you my lover,
and you pushed me out of your bed.
I called you my teacher,
and you didn't want me near you.
I called you my friend,
and you hurt my feelings for fun.

Now I hear you say "I love you,"
but I know you're lying.
I hear you talk about brotherhood,
but you clearly disdain me.
And when you say, "Our lives are precious..."
I want to ask, why is it, then,
that my life means nothing to you?

don Charles

138

Your mind is so narrow, I can't exist there.
Your behavior so arrogant, I can't stomach you.
Your cruelty so profound, I don't want your touch.
Your sincerity so trifling, I won't listen to you.

Look in my eyes, Black man,
and see mirrored there
the contempt with which you look at me.
Look behind the mirror,
and see the love that can't break through.

Should I call you:
Father?
Lover?
Teacher?
Friend?
Or should I scream:
Hypocrite!
Liar!
Bastard!
Son-of-a-bitch!

Should I embrace you?
Should I take your life?
Or should I just keep my distance?

All my life, I've been like a kaleidoscope.
In my parents' eyes, in my own eyes,
I have many images.
Turn the kaleidoscope,
and the image changes.

I

Shape of disappointment. Color of rejection.
In my father's eyes,
I'm the son he's not proud of.
A goody-two-shoes, too nice to say curse words.
A mama's boy, tied up tight in apron strings.
An impostor who looks like a man, but isn't.
Turn the kaleidoscope,
and the image changes.

II

Shape of disgust. Color of revulsion.
In my mother's eyes,
I'm the son she's ashamed of.
A stranger who buys gay magazines.
A pervert who couples with his own gender.
A health risk she's afraid of getting AIDS from.
Turn the kaleidoscope,
and the image changes.

III

Shape of unhappiness. Color of anxiety.
In my own eyes,
I'm a man who's broken inside.
A forced smile fading fast.
A cartoon character no longer funny.
A knit sweater that's beginning to unravel.
Turn the kaleidoscope,
and the image changes.

All my life, I've been like a kaleidoscope.
In my parents' eyes, in my own eyes,
I have many images.
Shapes I never wanted. Colors I never liked.
In the eyes of someone,
I want new images.

Shape of pride. Color of acceptance.
Shape of compassion. Color of welcome.
Shape of hope. Color of healing.

Turn, kaleidoscope!

IF HE HADN'T KISSED ME

And the fool said to me
as he humped my behind:
"You ought to try
fucking a woman sometime."

"Gotta have you some pussy
to be a *real* man,"
he said while I jacked him off
on my divan.

I wanted to ask him
to see if he knew:
"Why would I mess with
a jackass like you,
if pussy was what
I wanted to do?"

And if he hadn't kissed me,
I would have, too.

Suddenly at last, here I am in the cool shade.
People were pressing in on me,
and there was no place to be private
with my thoughts.

Damn that fool and his camera!
Damn those lovers who found each other so easily!
Damn those old Sunday ladies, walking so slow
and blocking my way to this cool, shady seat!

I'm dead, aren't I? Even though my life goes on.
My dreams went from me like rats
deserting a sinking ship,
and I died.
Now despair is a vulture tearing at my flesh.

But maybe I'll survive death.
Maybe I'll never hurt more than I hurt right now.

And maybe it will always be like this:
the fools clicking their cameras,
the lovers dripping saccharine,
the old ladies gossiping by the flowers,
the church bells sounding one more hour,
and me, here in the cool shade.

djola bernard branner

RED BANDANAS

Known best for his work with Pomo Afro Homos, DJOLA BERNARD BRANNER has toured nationally and internationally with *Fierce Love: Stories from Black Gay Life* and *Dark Fruit*. His writings are featured in several anthologies as well, including *In the Life* and most recently *The Road Before Us*. Branner appeared in Marlon Riggs' films, *Tongues Untied* and *Anthem*.

For daddy, who taught me to sing from the diaphragm.

Acknowledgments:
Some of these poems were published in *Bay Times, Five Fingers Review*, and *Clay Drum*.

RED BANDANAS

(as rapped to 101 b.p.m. minus—one)

mean fuck me
when worn
in the right
hip pocket
in the right crowd

on castro
or christopher
streets

but mine is worn
around the neck.

it means that
i am remembering
granddad
who wiped
the sweat from his
brow onto it
or used it to catch
the contents of
a cough
or laundered it/

and wore it around
his neck.

red bandanas

mean fuck me
when worn
in the right
hip pocket
in the right crowd

on castro
or christopher
streets

but mine is worn
around the neck.

it means that
i am remembering
moms
who placed it
in the palm of
my hand/
and dried
the tears she
cried in it
'cause her
father died
with nothing
but his/

red bandanas

mean fuck me
when worn
in the right
hip pocket
in the right crowd

on castro
or christopher
streets

but mine is worn
around the neck.

djola bernard branner   144

Pampers did not exist in '54
only Elvis/The Drifters
and all the fine Black men
who fell outta nightclubs
on South Central Avenue
like comets fall outta nighttime
sky/leaving sparks
bullets and babies
behind 'em.

It was catch
as catch can/so at sixteen
Darla's mother caught
what she could

a baby/

a frail thang
no more than four
pounds/something
she dropped quick
as a sprinter
drops a baton
into another runner's hand
and continues
with the relay

besides/Darla did not need much
even at four pounds
she could burp herself/almost
change her own diaper
except she couldn't snap
the safety pin.

There were no Pampers
in '54/only Darla

her mother who was too young
to mother and too grown-up
to be a daughter/
only Darla
who was quiet as stagnant water
and the furrow between her mother's eyes
only Darla
and all the restless boys
who'd watch her bosom
sprout overnight
her hips spread and split
like ripe plums
when they fall
from the tree.

At sixteen/the stagnant water
        in Darla's eyes
turned to steam
scalding every young blood
within their range

        — a fox man/a fuckin' star!

There was no way to dispute
it/the sky blushed
at twilight
and the sun dropped
from the sky
when Darla walked by

        — baby/you got to/got to
got to talk to me....

Every brother in South-Central
L.A. extended her a crown
along with a throbbing

djola bernard branner   146

heart
in his hand
'til Darla's mother
intervened

      — slut/whore
who gon' feed the nappy-headed
      so-and-so you bring in my house?

              *   *   *

Pampers did not exist in '70
only Smokey/The Moments
and Gordon
who was so fine
Darla couldn't look him
in the eye
      a jaw like Belafonte's
an air like Poitier's

and she fell like a river
from a mountain
into Gordon's arms/
bubbling right past her mother's
warning/and spilling
on into the sea.

Then she wept
like a willow
when the rabbit croaked
and Gordon leapt
away quicker than a hare.

There were no Pampers
in '70/only Darla
and the furrow between her

mother's eyes
which fell along with her
daughter's grace

    — well/   her mother said

well/as if Darla's confession
was a drop of rain
and her life had comprised a drought.

              *   *   *

Some things defy
common sense/
human determination
even prayer
only Darla
never understood
what she was never taught
but/ only Fate sometimes
will have its way.

NO SECRET

there is no secret
to my bending
twisting
buttocks writhing
forward
swiftly looping side
to side/
baby
i got soul.

I'M A WOMAN
(I'M A BACKBONE)

For Chaka Khan

I believed all the lyrics
you sang
like/thangs have been
going wrong
long enuf to know
everythang is right

and I'm a woman
(I'm a backbone)

were real
'cause you were always laughing
like a chorus
of exotic birds
or crying
like a fork
in the Nile

and I wish you had cried
more often Chaka
'cause then you wouldn't have been
snorting
and shooting
(who knows)
and smoking so much
and maybe I could say
right now
that I don't feel
betrayed.

We made love
some Saturdays
when my mother thought
I was singing
to pass the time
and keep from cleaning house

here to dare

your voice moved
into mine
like the sun moves
into dawn
defined the tone
the pitch
           the rise
                   the fall
and the end result
was always live.

Somebody say Chaka
and my name
was uttered
in the same breath
Bernard-and-Chaka
and Chaka-and-Bernard

and friends heard
me screaming
your name at concerts
           shouting/sing it girl
and yeah
baby
        ooow
               get down
and crawling all over
chairs to get
within view
of your Nubian eyes
but never touching you
(though I could have once)
'cause I would have known
you were flesh
and blood

and not a backbone
or a sweet thang
or any of the other words
your songs described
you as.

You were just trying
to make it
like the rest of us
laughing
when you could find the time
and trying to keep
from crying

and I wish you had cried
more often Chaka
'cause then you wouldn't have been
snorting
and shooting
(who knows)
and smoking so much
and maybe I could say
right now
that I don't feel
betrayed

and that I had not
betrayed you

believing you were a backbone
and not a woman.

large hands and
chipped nail polish
extended to reach the clock/
      lord   lord   another day
dial   set to kjlh   compton.
toes hunting high shag
for a pair of slippers/
      will need to light the furnace soon
morning dew
on barred windows
joints stiff with cold.
fingers through greasy hair
then lowered to relieve an itch/
      dreams   gotta call my son
      jus like his daddy that boy
      wit' his writin' writin'.
crooked picture of jesus christ
and marks on the wall
from repeated hangings/
      lord   let me heat some water
flannel robe gathered
and tied
as if someone will see.
linoleum floor and
slick sound of slippers
a blue flame   a copper kettle
and a bag of lipton tea/
      wear my navy pants
      and my light blue sweater,
      one my son gimme las' christmas.
      know he ain't up
      or i'd give him a call
muted roar of sliding closet
wire hangers and
tight rows of fabric/
don't need no ironin' either.
      ain't doin' nothin' but
      a white woman's wash.

djola bernard branner   152

eyes that smile   lips that tremble
boiling water and a stone cold iron/
        lord i'm movin' in circles today
        let me try that boy   no answer.
straightened picture
of jesus christ.

LISTEN

the bird's eye
never blinks
in Autumn/
least it miss
some signal
from God

he hands them out
like bread crumbs
to pigeons/
free
for the asking

to those who sit
still/and

listen.

i asked my boss
once
why he never hired
      any blacks
besides myself/
he threw his redneck back
billowed with laughter
and said it was bad enough
he had to contend with one/
      he told me
point blank
he has no intention
of putting another nigga
on payroll/and
      didn't even flinch
when i said that was discrimination.

so i have taken to
hiding my nigga side/
swallowing adjectives
that swish in my mouth/
refining my anger
so   that like
chinese needles
it cannot be felt
      when puncturing skin/
you know i cuddle
with my disdain at night
to quell it
      during the day/but
i wonder/
      sometimes
if the mental strain
is worth
the material gain.

djola bernard branner

POEM FOR ROBERT

(For his collection of photographs entitled Black Book*)*

thank you
mister mapplethorpe
for clicking the shutter
a' your magic
box

and catching
my brothers' smiles
bright enuf
to pale the sun
put glare in nighttime
sky
thanks for grabbing
hands thick enuf
to hold hurricanes
at bay
and barter wit' despair

thank you
mister mapplethorpe
for lassoing all a' my
crazy gazelle selves
and tying them
to 8 x 10 glossies

bless you
for crawling all up lean
calves
strong thighs
and size twelves
firm enuf
to stalk asphalt
and jungle-floor

we are moonlight
now
dancing offa
shoulder blades
catcall
spiraling
down kinky hair

we are ocelot
essence of the nile
no
we be antelope
black panther
brother-a-mine
we be one more
lean-mean-cheetah-
without-spots-
strutting-every-which-
a-way-on-god's-green-
earth

thank you
master picture-taker
sir
for reminding us of
who we are
my black brothers
and i
have lit a candle
for you
our images are blazing
eternally.

Would you buckle
  were you standing
when I read this poem
your stomach muscles
contract/your mouth
salivate

Would you shudder
were you still
  when I read this poem
your bones shatter/your flesh
fall to the ground

  My poems
are translations/a jagged
cliff the sea lopped
off in a tantrum
  the bark splintered
by a bolt of lightning
a liquid sliver of sunshine

My words
may envelop you
like a shawl
too scratchy for comfort
  too slight to combat
the cold/but

  My voice
ought to linger
like the melody
of a song.

djola bernard branner   156

INDEX OF TITLES

BOOKS AVAILABLE
FROM GALIENS PRESS

THE ROAD BEFORE US (100 GAY BLACK POETS), edited by Assoto Saint, $10.00. This provocative anthology celebrates in print one hundred poems, which are richly allusive, risk-taking and representing a wide range of voices. This unique collection is a must. The writers explore every aspect of gay Black life: from tradition to alienation, from the fierce gender-bending "vogue" culture to defiant sex and love in the age of AIDS, from historical and political perspectives to personal reflections. *The Road Before Us* was the winner of a 1991 Lambda Literary Award in the Gay Men's Poetry category. It was also nominated for a Gay/Lesbian Book Award by the American Library Association.

STATIONS, by Assotto Saint, $5.00. A cycle which traces the interracial love of two gay men as a celebration of survival, *Stations* stands as a "monumental testimony to the pain of experience and the beauty of love." The poems are stunning, painfully honest, richly crafted, and always full of surprises.

GALIENS PRESS
Box 4026
524 West 23rd Street
New York, NY 10011

Add $2.00 postage and handling for one book. For more than one book add an additional fifty cents per book. New York State residents please add appropriate sales tax. U.S. currency only. Personal checks or money orders please.

ABOUT THE EDITOR

Author of several theater pieces on the lives of gay. Black men, including *New Love Song* and *Risin' to the Love We Need*, ASSOTTO SAINT was born and raised in Haiti. He edited the anthology *The Road Before Us (100 Gay Black Poets),* which won a 1991 Lambda Literary Award in the Gay Men's Poetry category, and was nominated for a 1991 Gay/Lesbian Book Award by the American Library Association. His chapbook, *Triple Trouble*, was anthologized in *Tongues Untied* (GMP, London, 1987); his poetry collection, *Stations*, was published by Galiens Press in 1989. His writings have appeared in numerous anthologies and North American periodicals. He is a person with AIDS residing in New York City.